THE SOCIAL WORKER GRID®

THE SOCIAL WORKER GRID®

By

ROBERT R. BLAKE, Ph.D.

President
Scientific Methods, Inc.
Austin, Texas

JANE SRYGLEY MOUTON, Ph.D.

Vice-President
Scientific Methods, Inc.
Austin, Texas

LOUIS TOMAINO, D.S.W.

Dean
Worden School of Social Service
Our Lady of the Lake University
San Antonio, Texas

and

SHARON GUTIERREZ, M.S.W.

Private Practitioner
El Paso, Texas

CHARLES C THOMAS • PUBLISHER
Springfield • Illinois • U.S.A.

Published and Distributed Throughout the World by

CHARLES C THOMAS • PUBLISHER
Bannerstone House
301-327 East Lawrence Avenue, Springfield, Illinois, U.S.A.

ISBN 0-398-03915-1

Library of Congress Catalog Card Number: 79-10087

With THOMAS BOOKS *careful attention is given to all details of manufacturing and design. It is the Publisher's desire to present books that are satisfactory as to their physical qualities and artistic possibilities and appropriate for their particular use.* THOMAS BOOKS *will be true to those laws of quality that assure a good name and good will.*

Printed in the United States of America
V-R-1

Library of Congress Cataloging in Publication Data
Main entry under title:

The Social worker grid.

Includes index.
1. Social service. 2. Social workers.
I. Blake, Robert Rogers, 1918-
NV41.S6617 361.3'2 79-10087
ISBN 0-398-03915-1

PREFACE

THE objective of this book is to help social workers strengthen their social work practice. The focus is on the social worker in relationships with clients, whether individuals, families, or groups. The Social Worker Grid is a set of practical theories about relationships between social workers and their clients.

The historical distinction between an individual as the client and a group, such as a family, or even strangers who come together for discussion purposes, has become blurred in the recent past of social work. The reason is that few problems are solved by an individual without agreement, consultation, approval, or acceptance by others. Therefore, it is coming to be recognized that when an individual's actions affect someone else, he or she is a member of a group rather than a person who is able to act entirely in his or her own behalf. By recognizing this membership character, social work is coming to appreciate the importance of seeing an individual in the full context of day-to-day living.

Examples given have concentrated on the individual for purposes of clarity; the terms "casework" and "social work practice" are used interchangeably.

Robert R. Blake
Jane Srygley Mouton
Louis Tomaino
Sharon Gutierrez

CONTENTS

THE SOCIAL WORKER GRID®

Chapter 1

THE SOCIAL WORKER AND CLIENT GRIDS

SOCIAL work places considerable emphasis on *how* practitioners enter the lives of those they seek to help. Yet this does not always receive the examination it deserves in view of the many intervention methods that are possible. The Social Worker Grid seeks to clarify this intervention issue by starting with the following proposition: *Behavior, whether that of an individual in solitude, of people within a group, or in a larger social setting, tends to be cyclical in character. In other words, a sequence of behavior repeats its main features within specific time periods or within specifiable settings.*[1]

For example, an alcoholic may start each day with a drink. He may not start in exactly the same manner and time every day. He may depart from his drinking pattern in some way but these departures are only variations on a regular theme. Heroin addicts engage in the same regular patterns. Chronically aggressive or passive clients tend to repeat their actions in consistent ways wherever they find themselves. Ghetto residents become entrapped in day-to-day routines of the poverty cycle.

You may even agree that your own daily behavior is mainly cyclical. Many of your actions become habitual or are completed almost unconsciously. As long as this repetition stays within certain situational boundaries, it helps you achieve your daily tasks and succeed in what you are doing.

Cycle-Breaking Interventions

Outside these boundaries, however, an unreviewed behavior cycle can be harmful or destructive. This is frequently true of the clients you serve. The social worker's function, therefore, is

[1]Blake, R. R. and J. S. Mouton, *Consultation*. Reading, Mass.: Addison-Wesley Publishing Co., 1976, p. 2.

to assist the client in breaking out of damaging cycles. *An intervention occurs whenever a social worker does something with a client in the context of a cycle-breaking endeavor.* Who does what — with whom — for what purpose, of course, involves a whole spectrum of interactions. A therapist interprets a patient's "transference," hoping the patient can identify certain past feelings about the therapist or the boss back on the job. A juvenile probation officer points out certain legal consequences of delinquent behavior to a teenage client, hoping that the youngster can foresee how his or her actions might lead to loss of freedom.

Thus we are suggesting that caseworkers do not just intervene at large. From its earliest beginnings, social work has aimed at breaking the cyclical patterns clients have developed that keep them entrapped. Thinking of intervention in this manner enables you to see the Social Worker Grid in terms of which interventions are most likely to change a client's cycle, since the various Grid-oriented interventions all have fairly predictable consequences.

Agent of Change

Social work practitioners have always been aware of social change per se but have been hesitant to accept the idea of change being applied to individual clients in order to shift their behavior. The term *change* tends to foster mixed feelings in those caseworkers who may not like to think they are changing others. Therefore, words like education, training, or therapy are used in place of change because they seem more acceptable or comfortable. These words sound more consistent with traditional social work principles about client rights to self-determination and nonjudgmental attitudes of caseworkers. However, the fact remains that the social worker still intervenes to change the client.

The Social Worker Grid presents a different notion about change because it sees the caseworker as society's paid agent of change. This is particularly true when working in the public sector where the majority of social work is done.

When stripped to its most essential elements, the task of the caseworker is one of assisting individuals to rid themselves of disabling problems. Thus, by adopting a change perspective and redefining the caseworker as an agent of change, it may become possible to gain insight into why various caseworkers see their work as they do and to actually evaluate their assumptions systematically within a change theory context. At the same time, you might be able to apply theory and research about how change can take place in your job.

The Social Worker Grid

When you are involved with a client, at least two thoughts are in your mind: concern for the client's problem and concern for the client as a person. These can be represented graphically in a diagram consisting of two scales. The way these two concerns mesh determines your social work style.

What does *concern for* mean? It does not indicate "how much." Rather, it indicates the character and strength of the assumptions present behind any given style. What is significant is the degree to which a caseworker is concerned about a client's problem and the degree he or she is concerned about the client as a person, and how these two concerns are intertwined.

Concern for problem solving and concern for the client are expressed in different ways, depending on how these two concerns meet. That is, high concern for solving the problem which joins a low concern for the client is very different from the kind of high problem-solving concern that joins with high concern for the client. In this context, the social worker's concern for the client is at the foundation of his or her casework strategy.

Figure 1 shows these concerns and the ways they interact.[2] The horizontal axis indicates concern for solving the client's problem; the vertical axis indicates concern for the client as a person. Each is expressed on a nine-point scale: *1* represents minimal concern, *5* symbolizes an intermediate degree of con-

---

[2]The literature of behavioral science research on which the Grid is based includes about 400 references. The sources of these references are Blake, R. R. and J. S. Mouton, *The Managerial Grid.* Houston: Gulf Publishing Co., 1964; and Blake, R. R. and J. S. Mouton, *The New Managerial Grid.* Houston: Gulf Publishing Co., 1978.

cern, and *9* represents maximal concern. They do not stand for any literal amounts but signify positions rather like empty or half full on your automobile gas gauge. The other numbers, *2* through *4* and *6* through *8* denote an uninterrupted sequence of successive degrees of concern.

In the lower right corner is the 9,1-oriented social worker. Here, high concern for problem solving is coupled with little or no concern for the client as a person. Clients are seen as motivated to change only when they have to. The caseworker's job is to make sure they know what is expected of them and to ensure that clients live up to these expectations. This caseworker puts pressure on a client and is mainly a *controller* of

The Social Worker Grid®

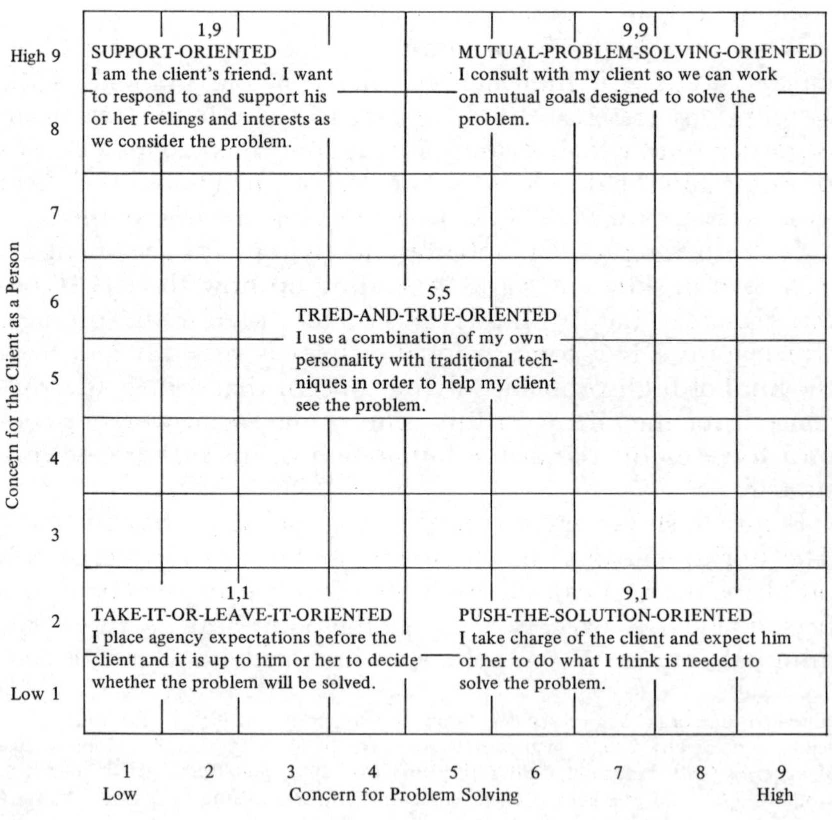

Figure 1

what is happening in the casework process. The caseworker believes that problems are more likely to be solved in this way regardless of what the client feels as an individual. This way of behavior has its own unique motivations. There are two sides to this motivational coin involving what a person seeks to realize and what he or she wants to avoid. We examine both sides later in the context of each Grid style.

The 1,9 approach is shown in the upper left corner. Here a minimum concern for problem solving joins a maximum concern for the client. Under this style, little direct influence is used with the client. The caseworker is interested primarily in the client's feelings and seeks to develop a friendly relationship with the client. The caseworker believes that client change occurs when insight is gained via a warm, supportive, nondirective, and nonjudgmental relationship. The social worker tends to function mainly as a client-centered *therapist* in the casework process.

At the lower left corner is the 1,1 strategy. The caseworker's concern for problem solving and concern for clients are both at a low ebb. This leads to passive behavior. Assuming this posture, the caseworker thinks that clients really do not change as a result of casework. Therefore, the caseworker "goes through the motions" and contributes little to the interactions that occur with clients, believing that "it is up to them." Here the caseworker emerges mainly as an *observer* of what happens.

In the center is the 5,5 approach, a middle-of-the-road strategy containing an intermediate amount of both concerns. This is based on the idea that the caseworker tries to strike some balance between problem solving and client concern, inasmuch as it is unrealistic to think that one can attain both of these ends simultaneously. This social worker relies on a methodical, conservative set of casework routines and techniques to get results.

Finally, in the upper right corner is the 9,9 strategy where high concern for problem solving and high concern for the client are integrated. Here the social worker helps the client change through aiding him or her in the selection of available options that can be tested until the client's dysfunctional cycle is broken and replaced with more effective behavior. Concern for the client is demonstrated through the caseworker asking questions such as — Can what I and my agency bring be really useful to the client? What benefits does all this have for the client? How can I actively involve the client in setting goals? 9,9 represents a deep concern for the client's interests and for the change the client will experience as a result of successful casework.

The Grid positions will be described more fully in subsequent chapters as each demonstrates a different style employed in everyday casework. Other social worker styles can be shown on the Grid. Eighty-one different combinations of these two concerns, such as 8,3 or 5,7, might be represented in a two scale nine-point system. Our study, however, is based on analyzing the corner and middle Grid positions according to the theories and strategies of social work they symbolize, because these are the most important theories of casework.

Does a social worker simply set up assumptions and associated strategies or does he or she skip over the surface of the Grid, shifting and adapting according to how the situation is seen? Actually, most caseworkers have a dominant Grid style which is supported by backup Grid styles. There are five major social worker Grid styles, but the number of possible dominant plus backup combinations, as well as other mixtures of Grid strategies, is quite large. We will deal more extensively with these dynamics in Chapter 8.

In a way, social worker effectiveness can be developed as an applied behavioral science. It is the caseworker's artistic skill in sensing the nuances, biases, and emotional colors which affects the casework interaction.

Assumptions and Grid Positions

Each of the five caseworker theories is based on a different set of assumptions. Each points to a fundamentally different way of orienting oneself to the job of casework: *Assumptions* are things a person takes for granted as being true or reliable in producing an effect.[3] They are at the core of your customary

[3]The role of assumptions in guiding behavior is widely recognized in the behavioral sciences. Typical are Bion, W. R. *Experience in Groups*. New York: Basic Books, McGraw-Hill, 1959; McGregor, D. *The Human Side of Enterprise*. New York:

social work strategy. If you interacted with a client without making assumptions about what was going to produce some change, you would have no caseworker strategy at all! Your behavior would be purposeless. Even so, it is not enough just to have a set of assumptions. Faulty assumptions can lead to ineffective casework. People do not often question their basic assumptions, but it is a way of checking out your casework and examining alternative assumptions that might make you more effective.

Different sets of assumptions lead to a whole range of different casework outcomes that range from highly effective to very ineffective. If you can identify your most natural assumptions, you can also identify what kind of casework results follow from their use. Similarly, the effects of other sets of assumptions can be traced through to their likely results. Then you will have an opportunity to check different assumptions against your own. If you wish to change some of your own assumptions, you will be in a position to do so.

Clients or other social workers who observe caseworkers might think of their Grid style as personality, yet these five theories do not define *personality* characteristics. They indicate anchor positions for one's basic assumptions out of which particular attitudes and practices emerge. They are not meant to suggest that an individual social worker is a fixed type or to be viewed as a label for people. Yet, for some caseworkers, the Grid style they use is deeply embedded as a way of interacting with others. It has become their customary way of operating.

Social workers can learn how to change their behavior by making use of different assumptions. That is why this book can be useful to you. It provides an opportunity to identify the casework assumptions under which you now operate. It can help you examine alternative assumptions and how these undergird different casework strategies. Once you can identify what reduces your casework effectiveness, you are progressing toward making a change in the direction of greater effective-

---

McGraw-Hill, 1960, pp. 6-8; Steiner, C. M. *Scripts People Live: Transactional Analysis of Life Scripts.* New York: Bantam, 1974, pp. 59-111; Dreikurs, R. and L. Grey, *Logical Consequences: A New Approach to Discipline.* New York: Meredith Press, 1968, pp. 23-27; Barber, J. D. *The Presidential Character: Predicting Performance in the White House.* Englewood Cliffs, N. J.: Prentice-Hall, 1972, pp. 7-9.

ness. Once you see how much more effective you can be by doing something different, your progress in casework effectiveness can accelerate. Thus, the emphasis throughout this book is on introspection and self-appraisal.

Your primary interest is to help the client break out of a dysfunctional cycle through casework processes. Basic forces at work in case situations, which help determine the change approach you employ, come from —

1. immediate situations, i.e. time pressures, resistance from your supervisor, high caseloads, etc.;
2. your own Grid style;
3. your client's Grid style;
4. requirements (real or imagined) of your agency such as agency rules, past practices, or mission of the agency.

Of all of these forces, the one you can most readily do something about is yourself. The one you can next most readily influence is the client. The assumptions the client reveals in dealing with you as a caseworker can also be identified to aid you in understanding your client.

The Client Grid

Now let us take an X ray of the situation from the perspective of the client. A client also has two concerns: a concern for solving his or her problem, shown along the horizontal axis of the Client Grid, and a concern for the caseworker as a person, shown on the vertical axis. Each of these two concerns also ranges from low to high. Depending on how they come together, they reveal five basic Grid style orientations to the client's assumptions, strategies, and ways of interacting with the caseworker.

In the lower right corner is the 9,1-oriented client whose main concern is for dealing with the problem in his or her own way. Little concern is present for you as the caseworker. The attitude is "This caseworker will take advantage of me if I allow it, so I must stay in control." This client tends to have a closed mind and strong convictions. Although the client may not have a clear idea of what his or her needs are, this individual is not willing to admit that you may be able to help.

The Client Grid®

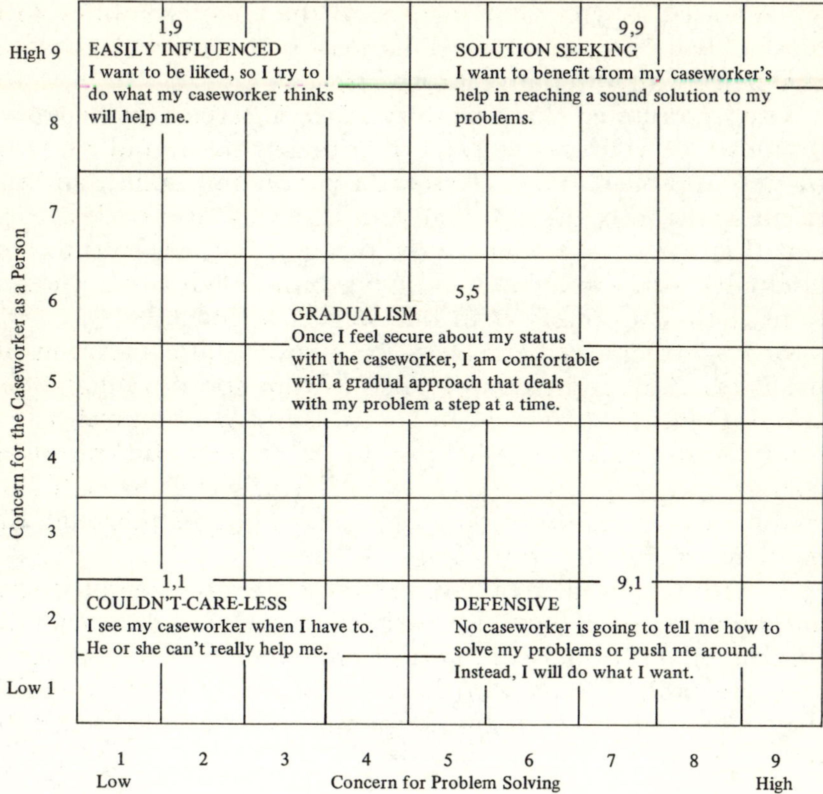

Figure 2

The attitude is "I am going to stand up for my rights." He or she become impatient easily, resisting change, blocking your efforts, and turning the casework process into a win-lose battle.

A 1,9-oriented client has little real concern for solving the problem but a high concern for you. This individual's deep desire is to be accepted and approved of, resulting in him or her being easily influenced by you. This client's attitude is "I want to do whatever you think best."

When a client is characterized by 1,1 assumptions, with little concern for either problem solving or for you as caseworker, the typical attitude is "Social workers try but they can't really help. I do only what's necessary." Reactions to you are usually perfunctory and disinterested. When the client does respond, it is the path of least resistance. Appointments are kept, activities are reported to you, and in general the client complies with most of your expectations. This person has no real gut-level convictions about change prospects.

The 5,5-oriented client tends to make uncertain and tentative responses to your casework efforts, preferring a gradual, step-by-step approach. Your reputation is very important, and the client wants to be assured that your casework approach is tried and true. He or she wants to be pleasant but responds to you gradually, so as to avoid complying blindly with your suggestions if they are more than one step at a time.

The 9,9-oriented client seeks to discover sound solutions to problems. This individual is open to your specific suggestions and responds positively when you consult with him or her in a candid manner. The client looks for facts and valid reasons to change and will more likely do so if you come through as a credible caseworker, not only as a person but also through the message or content you offer.

As with the Social Worker Grid, there are more combinations and mixtures than these five basic client styles, but they are the fundamental sets of assumptions from which more complicated ones are built. Clients also have backup Grid styles to which they move whenever their dominant style can no longer be relied upon.

When Social Worker and Client Meet

A step toward gaining greater skill as a caseworker can now be taken. Let us begin to study how the Grid styles of caseworkers and clients interact in their efforts to bring about change. The character of interactions between a social worker and a client determines whether there is a successful outcome.

There are combinations of social worker and client styles that can result in negative casework outcomes. Other combinations seem to "fit" and promote more effective casework with good mutual understanding and respect between caseworker and client. We will try to determine, in a general way, which Social Worker Grid styles are likely to be effective or ineffective when the caseworker is facing clients with different Grid styles. Com-

Effectiveness of Grid Styles

Social Worker Grid Style	Client Grid Style				
	1,1	1,9	5,5	9,1	9,9
9,9	+	+	+	+	+
9,1	0	+	+	0	0
5,5	0	+	+	–	0
1,9	–	+	0	–	0
1,1	–	–	–	–	–

Figure 3

binations of caseworker and client Grid styles are shown in Figure 3 in which the plus (+) means "likely to be effective," and zero (0) indicates "intermediate between effective and ineffective," and a minus (–) stands for "likely to be ineffective in producing change results."

These judgments cannot be absolute because of the many variables that influence casework. The general trends shown are the best predictions in the light of current knowledge.[4] The more subtle complexities between caseworkers and clients will be examined in detail in later chapters.

Finally, there is reason to believe that the Social Worker's Grid may be more crucial for change induction than the client's. The caseworker, by virtue of what he or she does or does not do, is in the best position to set the climate for change in the relationship. The kind of climate the caseworker creates as a leader is likely to cause the client to react in kind.

[4]Current scholarly evaluations of the Grid as a strategy for comprehending and changing superior-subordinate relationships are available in a number of sources. See Huse, E. F. and J. L. Bowditch, *Behavior in Organizations: A Systems Approach to Managing,* 2nd ed. Reading, Mass.: Addison-Wesley, 1977; Todes, J. L., J. McKinney, and W. Ferguson, Jr. *Management and Motivation: An Introduction to Supervision.* New York: Harper & Row, 1977; Sanford, A. C., G. T. Hunt, and H. J. Bracey, *Communication Behavior in Organizations.* Columbus, Ohio: Charles E. Merrill Publishing Company, 1976; Cribbin, J. J. *Effective Managerial Leadership.* New York: American Management Association, Inc., 1972; Harris, O. J., Jr. *Managing People at Work.* New York: John Wiley & Sons, Inc., 1976; Tubbs, S. L. and S. Moss, *Human Communication,* 2nd ed. New York: Random House, 1974.

Mandino has captured this notion in this passage addressed to salesmen:

> Trees and plants depend on the weather to flourish but I make my own weather, yea I transport it with me. If I bring rain and gloom and darkness and pessimism and they will purchase naught. If I bring joy and enthusiasm and brightness and laughter to my customers, they will react with joy and enthusiasm and brightness and laughter and my weather will produce a harvest of sales and a granary of gold for me.[5]

This is important. It indicates that the caseworker *can* be a leader if he or she knows how. The client can be taught sound behavioral change. This is what creates a good relationship and mutual respect and brings about a solution to the client's problem.

---

[5]Mandino, O. G. *The Greatest Salesman in the World.* New York: Bantam Books, 1968, pp. 79-80.

Chapter 2

SEE YOURSELF IN THE SOCIAL WORKER GRID MIRROR

BEFORE getting into the minute-by-minute activities involved in casework, let us take a quick glance at you. This can help you look beneath the surface and see yourself as a person with a dominant Grid style.

Grid Elements*

Six elements describe qualities of personal behavior through which you can see your own Grid assumptions. These elements are decisions, convictions, conflict, temper, humor, and effort.

Five different sentences are provided under each element. Consider each sentence as a possible description of yourself in relation to that element. Place a *5* beside the sentence you think is most like yourself, the *actual* you, not the ideal you. Be as honest as you can.

Place a *4* beside the sentence you think is next most like yourself. Continue ranking the other sentences with *3* for the third, *2* for the fourth, and *1* for the fifth place, which is that sentence *least* characteristic of you. There can be no ties.

Element 1: Decisions

___ A1. I accept the decisions of clients with indifference.
___ B1. I support decisions that promote good relations.
___ C1. I search for workable, even though not perfect, decisions.
___ D1. I expect decisions I make to be treated as final.
___ E1. I place high value on getting sound creative decisions that result in understanding and agreement.

Reaching a decision is fundamental to any action. The point

*These elements are from *The Grid Seminar Prework. The Managerial Grid: An Exploration of Key Managerial Orientations.* Austin, Texas: Scientific Methods, Inc., 1962 (revised 1972).

where a person is committed to one course of action or another indicates the degree of certainty in making that choice. A person who can look at a situation, read the facts, and reach a decision is seen as confident in his or her ability to solve problems. This confidence promotes confidence in others. A person who is "wishy-washy" increases other's uncertainty regarding his or her own soundness.

Element 2: Convictions

___ A2. I avoid taking sides by not revealing opinions, attitudes, and ideas.
___ B2. I embrace opinions, attitudes, and ideas of clients rather than pushing my own.
___ C2. When others hold ideas, opinions, or attitudes different from my own, I try to meet them halfway.
___ D2. I stand up for my ideas, opinions, and attitudes, even though it sometimes results in stepping on toes.
___ E2. I listen for and seek out ideas, opinions, and attitudes different from my own. I have clear convictions but respond to ideas sounder than my own by changing my mind.

In a society where people are expected to think for themselves, the most highly respected are those who have sound convictions and hold to them. When a person has clear convictions, life has a sense of purpose, character, and direction. Individuals without convictions appear to others as weak, insecure, uncertain, anxious, or simply indifferent to real issues.

Element 3: Conflict

___ A3. When conflict arises, I try to remain neutral.
___ B3. I try to avoid generating conflict; when it does appear, I try to soothe feelings to keep people together.
___ C3. When conflict arises, I try to find fair solutions that accommodate others.
___ D3. When conflict arises, I try to cut it off or try to win my position.
___ E3. When conflict arises, I try to identify reasons for it and seek to resolve underlying causes.

Disagreement and conflict are inevitable in a culture where people have different points of view and readily express them. Conflict can be either disruptive and destructive or creative and constructive, depending upon how it is met and handled. A person who can face conflict with another and resolve it to mutual understanding evokes respect and admiration. Inability to cope with conflict constructively and creatively leads to disrespect or oftentimes to increased hostility and antagonism. One makes a relationship; the other breaks it.

Element 4: Temper

___ A4. By remaining uninvolved, I rarely get stirred up.
___ B4. Because of the disapproval tensions can produce, I react in a warm and friendly way.
___ C4. Under tension, I feel unsure and anxious about how to meet others' expectations.
___ D4. When things are not going right, I defend, resist, and come back with counterarguments.
___ E4. When aroused, I contain myself even though my impatience is visible.

Temper is an emotional reaction to stress, tension, and strain. Loss of temper means that reason has been abandoned and violent, negative emotions have taken over. The loss of temper also has contagious effects. Its destructive qualities can spread like wildfire. But when an individual maintains a steady head and a strong hand, others have confidence that this person relies on reason and they respect his or her leadership. Persons who withhold their involvement and concern to keep from being stirred up are suspect. They may even be seen as not understanding the urgency of the problem.

Element 5: Humor

___ A5. My humor is seen as rather pointless.
___ B5. My humor shifts attention away from the serious side.
___ C5. My humor sells me or my position.
___ D5. My humor is hard-hitting.
___ E5. My humor fits the situation and gives perspective; I retain a sense of humor even under pressure.

Humor brings perspective to situations of strain and impasse, as well as giving richness to contradictory events. A person with sound humor contributes to the enjoyment of others. A person who is humorless is seen as lifeless and having no fun. One brings people toward him or her; the other lets them walk away.

Element 6: Effort

___ A6. I put out enough to get by.
___ B6. I prefer to support others rather than initiate action.
___ C6. I seek to maintain a steady pace.
___ D6. I drive myself and others.
___ E6. I exert vigorous effort and others join in.

Healthy people have the capacity for using their energy in positive and constructive ways. When they do, enthusiasm is contagious; others catch it. It produces a "Can do!" spirit of optimism and progress. When they do not have enthusiasm, life is drab and conversation is dull and boring. Then pessimism creeps in, hopelessness appears, and a sense of "Why try?" results.

Your Grid Style

Figure 4 aids you in summarizing your rankings to answer the question, "What Grid style is most typical of me?" Start with the Decisions Element. Copy your rankings in row 1. Copy your rankings for the Convictions Element in Row 2, and so on. Then add up the score in each column.

The highest possible number for any Grid style is 30. This means that you were completely consistent in picking the same Grid style from all six elements. The Grid style on which you have the highest number is what you see as your dominant style. The one with the next highest is what you see as your backup. The Grid style with the lowest number represents the theory which you reject most strongly as representing you. The strongest possible rejection of a style is represented by a number 6.

Summary of Personal Rankings

Element	Grid Style				
	1,1	1,9	5,5	9,1	9,9
1 Decisions	A1 _____	B1 _____	C1 _____	D1 _____	E1 _____
2 Convictions	A2 _____	B2 _____	C2 _____	D2 _____	E2 _____
3 Conflict	A3 _____	B3 _____	C3 _____	D3 _____	E3 _____
4 Temper	A4 _____	B4 _____	C4 _____	D4 _____	E4 _____
5 Humor	A5 _____	B5 _____	C5 _____	D5 _____	E5 _____
6 Effort	A6 _____	B6 _____	C6 _____	D6 _____	E6 _____
Total	_____	_____	_____	_____	_____

Figure 4

Remember, this is a self-description. It may not represent the "true" you because most of us are prone to self-deception. However, it is a point of departure to keep in mind as you read through the book. You will want to rerank yourself after you have a greater understanding of Grid styles and of your own particular approach to casework.

At this point there are two questions you might be asking: "Are all the elements equally important in making up a caseworker's Grid style?" "Are there no other equally important elements?"

The answer to the first question is "no." They are not of equal importance. The Conflict Element appears to be the most central. You will see how important conflict is in the casework situation when you often must deal with objections, resistances, and complaints, or with clients who say one thing and do another, and so on. When you know a person's reaction to conflict, you tend to find that other elements fall in place around that reaction. That is why it is most important.

Are there other elements that make up a person's character? Yes, of course. Take for example such matters as one's personal integrity and thoroughness in pursuing knowledge, both about the immediate problem itself and about the client's approach to life. In later chapters, it will be seen that these aspects of a person's basic Grid style also are of significance.

The six elements presented here are fundamental for clear understanding of the assumptions that caseworkers make. They are also foundation stones for understanding the personal characteristics of a client.

We are now ready for an in-depth study of each Social Worker Grid style. In the next five chapters we examine the pure casework strategies from two broad perspectives. The first perspective in each chapter deals with the motivational dynamics which underlie the particular Grid positions being studied. The second assesses the path which your change efforts are likely to take as a result of the motivational dynamics at play. In Chapter 8 the various Grid mixtures and backup strategies are investigated. A chapter that evaluates the Client Grid in greater detail follows.

As you read, place yourself in as many of these situations being illustrated as you possibly can. Imagine the situation or consider what your reactions might be. Then you can check back and forth to see how your reactions square with the quantitative data you developed about yourself in this chapter. Keep in mind that "the focus of social work practice is on the interactions between people and systems in the social environment."[1]

---

[1]Pincus, A. and A. Minahan, *Social Work Practice: Model and Method.* Itasca, Illinois: F. E. Peacock Inc., 1973.

Chapter 3

9,1-ORIENTED SOCIAL WORKERS

THE 9,1-oriented caseworker is high on problem solving and low on concern for the client. The caseworker takes for granted that the client will only change when pressured to do so, and he or she has little reluctance about pushing solutions onto the client in order to control everything that happens.[1]

Motivational Dynamics

There is a positive and a negative side in a 9,1 approach to casework. On the positive side of a 9,1 motivational orientation, the social worker strives to be powerful, to control, and to dominate the client. This individual is driven to impose his or her will on the client and becomes angry when these efforts are frustrated. A caseworker motivated in this way is likely to respond to clients by demanding that whatever steps are needed for "success" be taken. This inflexible determination leaves the caseworker unmindful of the client as an individual.

The negative motivation, that is, what a 9,1-oriented caseworker seeks to avoid, is failure of not being able to straighten out the client's problem situation, and therefore being faced with defeat. This individual seeks to avoid failure by applying greater and greater persistence.

If you are operating under 9,1 motivations, you see yourself as the cause of whatever success comes your way, but you attribute failure to the client's reluctance, blockages created by the agency, and so on. Though you see others as the "cause" of your failures, this only results in your trying to dominate, master, and control your next client even more completely.

Now we can explore how a 9,1 orientation occurs in social

[1]The behavior and concerns of "inner directed" men at work as described by Riesman are characteristic of 9,1 assumptions and actions. See Riesman, D. *The Lonely Crowd.* New Haven: Yale University, 1961, pp. 111-126.

work practice.

SCENE: Social worker's office in large department of Public Welfare, Child Welfare Unit, 8:30 AM.

SOCIAL WORKER: Have a seat, Mrs. Blair. As you know, your two children are in Children's Shelter and are going to stay there until I am completely satisfied that you can be a better mother.

MRS. BLAIR: I am a good mother, I nearly went crazy looking for the children and . . .

SOCIAL WORKER: I don't understand that because I tried to contact you and could not find you.

MRS. BLAIR: I have a lot of problems; sometimes things get away from me but that doesn't mean I'm not a good mother.

SOCIAL WORKER: Yes, I know but I have an obligation to those kids. You will have to prove to me that they are going to get better care.

MRS. BLAIR (heatedly): They do get good care.

SOCIAL WORKER: You just settle down or you will get into more trouble than you already are. I am going to see that this matter is settled properly, and you are absolutely going to have to shape up or the consequences will be bad for you. Now, you will have to comply with the following four points which I am drawing up before you can expect to prove yourself to me.

This brief episode gives you a sense of how a 9,1-oriented social worker operates. The caseworker's primary concern in this situation is to solve the problem according to his or her prescription. No hint is made about the client's internal commitment to anything. Whether she likes it or not (and we see that she does not) she must "shape up or ship out."

If you are a 9,1-oriented social worker you will think that Mrs. Blair is not going to follow through on good care for the kids unless you *make* her comply. In this instance, the caseworker comes across as assuming Mrs. Blair is guilty and obviously needs someone to lead her. Mrs. Blair needs clear, firm direction, and only compliance with the caseworker will be satisfactory behavior. Given this perspective, the 9,1-oriented caseworker is interested in Mrs. Blair's children and feels responsible for helping but only on his or her terms.

You, as a caseworker, may recall times when you have become a controller in your own casework practice. If you are a student preparing yourself for social work, you may recall situations when you have done this with brothers or sisters or friends who sought your help or appeared to need it. Control, in itself, is not an evil to be avoided; it is necessary in modern complex living. The problem is in control that is imposed in a unilateral way and provokes resentment and resistance on the client's part.

Social Worker Behaviors

9,1-oriented caseworkers drive themselves and their clients in line with the ethic that "results are what counts." Whenever a contradiction exists between problem solving and working with the client as a person, it is resolved at the expense of the client. The caseworker's determination is to overcome obstacles. He or she believes strongly that if control is not exercised over the entire client situation, it will get out of hand because the client has already demonstrated the inability to solve his or her own problems.

When you function as a 9,1-oriented social worker, your responsibilities are expressed in the following way.

> PLANNING. "I do the planning by setting goals for my clients to follow."
>
> ORGANIZING. "I get my clients going by telling them what to do, when, and how."
>
> DIRECTING. "I keep close tabs on what is happening on a case-by-case basis."
>
> CONTROLLING. "I make sure that my clients are performing by double checking and imposing corrective actions quickly when the need for these becomes evident. I have no reluctance to criticize when the situation demands it."

Under these circumstances, a 9,1-oriented social worker is bent on compliance by the client. If the client complies, even though against his or her will, the caseworker might feel that at least the problem may be partly solved.

Casework can be assessed from several angles, but let us examine it from five points and return to the encounter with Mrs.

Blair. The five aspects of casework that are important for us to consider are (1) the importance of focus, (2) the uses which caseworkers make of their power, (3) the dependence of the client on the caseworker, (4) what happens with interviewing and recording, and (5) the personality of the agency.

Focus

Your ability to focus on your client as an individual is one of the most important skills a caseworker can possess. What does this mean? It means that you invest your energy in the client. This results in the client feeling important at that given time.

9,1-oriented social workers do not function this way. Notice in the above scene the focus was on the caseworker as the most important person in the situation. Statements like "until I am completely satisfied" and "you are going to have to prove to me. . ." diverted attention away from the client and onto the caseworker. The caseworker's needs and thoughts assume greater significance than those of the client. Under this orientation, you do most of the talking, using many terms like "ought," "should," "as everybody knows," "definitely," and "I think." By way of demonstrating your strength, you use various success examples from your own life. You insist on getting answers to every question, regardless of whether the client is ready to cooperate.

When a 9,1-oriented social worker fails to focus on the client, chances to get client involvement and to promote readiness to change can be lost. When Mrs. Blair said "Yes, I know but I have an obligation to those kids," this was an opportunity for the caseworker to find out more about Mrs. Blair, her children, and the problems as she had experienced them. Instead, the caseworker chose to present his or her own position rather than focus on Mrs. Blair and her problem in a way that could establish rapport and stimulate her to reexamine her own assumptions about herself, her children, and her problems.

Power Uses

The 9,1-oriented social worker has the power position and

feels he or she must keep it. When Mrs. Blair reacts a little heatedly she is told "you just settle down or you will get into more trouble." She is also told that there are four points to which she must agree without any regard for whether Mrs. Blair considers them to be reasonable. These are examples of how 9,1-oriented caseworkers use their power at the expense of concern for the client's feelings, involvement, participation, and commitment to problem solving.

If you use power in 9,1-oriented ways, you are not sharing it in any manner. You have a vested interest in your own position. You possess power by virtue of your status. When the client gives you a little trouble you react aggressively. When plans or goals are drawn up, you formulate them and tell the client how to go about their attainment. This, of course, is a unilateral use of power. Whatever success you have in changing the client rests on your power over him or her.

Change via compliance requires a relatively formal and well-defined power differential between you and your client. You rely heavily on "legalized" change and fall back on agency policy, regulations, statutes, etc., to enforce your power. Client commitment becomes impractical in view of what you think is the natural resistance of people to change.

Conflict arises when the caseworker's thinking contradicts that of the client or vice versa. A 9,1-oriented approach views conflict as an indication that control is breaking down in the casework process and steps must be taken to avoid this. Therefore, a 9,1-oriented caseworker reacts by trying to eliminate conflict with clients before it arises. This caseworker may put clients on the defensive very quickly by taking a fixed position on what he or she thinks the client ought to be doing.

Sometimes conflict erupts and then the caseworker is faced with open disagreement and a contest of wills. When this happens, the caseworker is out to win at all costs. One way is to suppress the conflict by cutting it off. How is this done? "Please don't say another word. Listen and repeat to me what I am about to tell you. . ." If this fails the caseworker may say "There is the door. You can just leave if you are not prepared to do as I have outlined."

If you are a 9,1-oriented social worker you do not hesitate to show emotions. These may range from anger, to scolding, through official congratulations to a client who is doing exactly as instructed.

An ultimate win-lose tactic is to pull rank on a client. For example, let's say that Mr. Jones, a sixty-six-year-old black man, comes into your agency seeking emergency housing because he has just been evicted from his apartment. This is an emergency situation and you react by stating "I think I can get you into the housing project in about two days." Mr. Jones responds angrily to this, saying "All you social workers are alike. Right away you think I should go into a housing project. No white man ever understood a black person anyway. I don't want a housing project and I think your idea is lousy."

The 9,1-oriented caseworker's reaction to this unexpected event is "Now you just wait one minute! Don't try and tell me what I feel and know about blacks. I've always been a sympathetic supporter of the black people and I demonstrated this in the 1960s. What were you doing in those days? Here I offer you a solution to the problem and you attack me without even knowing about me. Maybe you should go find your own place to live as you don't want what I have to offer. Go get your help elsewhere if that is the way you feel, and I advise you to go in with a different attitude."

The obvious thing here is that the caseworker has imposed his or her will on Mr. Jones. To accept Mr. Jones' point of view would expose the caseworker to the risk of failure. Mr. Jones must now knuckle under or leave. He has lost. This kind of suppression is often effective in ending conflict but it fails to get to the core of the problem. The real issue — one of housing need — takes a back seat to the power struggle that occurred.

In this situation, the social worker also used the technique of leverage to force compliance. If Mr. Jones does not comply he must simply leave — a worse consequence for him because he may receive no help. Other examples include threatening to cut off a welfare grant or suggesting that the caseworker will recommend termination of parental rights in a court hearing over children.

Dependence

The dependence variable may work in different ways during 9,1-oriented casework. On one hand 9,1-oriented social workers deplore dependent clients; they view these clients as weak and unable to fend for themselves. On the other hand, 9,1-oriented caseworkers may unwittingly encourage client dependency when they take over the problem by planning everything for the client. If you do this, you see clients as in need of a strong leader, a role which you can play. If clients do not resist your firm-handedness, they may in fact begin to rely on you rather than increase their self-reliance. You end up promoting the dependency reaction you detest. If Mrs. Blair wants her children back today, she must demonstrate enough dependency on her caseworker's prescriptions to convince the worker that she will act according to the caseworker's expectations. If she does, she can expect help from her strong and knowing caseworker. The 9,1-oriented caseworker strives diligently to solve a problem but in anticipation of appropriate client responses of a dependent, compliant kind.

Interviewing and Recording

Good record keeping and interview procedure are important for effective casework, but the character of interviewing and recording is influenced by the caseworker's Grid style.

9,1-oriented caseworkers feel most secure when they are in charge of the interview. Accordingly, interview dynamics are highly structured with regard to time, place, and circumstances. There is some preoccupation with who is on top of the verbal exchange. Little or no silence occurs, many direct questions are asked, and notes are taken, thoroughly and minutely.

Accurate record keeping and documentation of detail are more crucial than the content of client feelings. Therefore, a 9,1-oriented caseworker insists on getting answers to every question regardless of whether the client is ready to cooperate. You are likely to make the client "sweat a little" in your attempt to "catch" him or her in contradictions, being careful to substantiate all this in comprehensive recording.

When reviewing client records, a 9,1-oriented caseworker stresses facts and information rather than diagnostic interpretation of what is important in the client's situation. The caseworker points out that Mrs. Blair was the fourth of nine children in her own family, quit school in the ninth grade, and claimed that her mother nagged at her as a teenager. However, little analysis is done as to what it meant to Mrs. Blair to have been in a large family or to have left school early, or what her present feelings are about teenage life patterns.

A 9,1-oriented caseworker records that Mr. and Mrs. Blair were married on 10-12-65, that the children were born on 9-11-66, 8-8-67, 12-13-69, and that the father abandoned them on 1-14-70. These records are factual and thorough but do not reflect real people. "Life stuff" gets buried in chronology, and the relationships between facts or events receive no emphasis. All of this reflects high concern for the problem but low concern for the client as a person.

An alternative way of recording the information in the 9,9-orientation follows: "Mr. and Mrs. Blair married when both were eighteen and had three children within four years, apparently causing important emotional and economic strains. When Mr. Blair left the family shortly after birth of the third child, Mrs. Blair felt extremely rejected and didn't know where to turn for help."

Agency Personality

It is true that social service agencies develop their own environments and reflect these to clients in various ways. This adds up to what we call the personality, or culture, of an agency.

Let us consider briefly what a 9,1-oriented agency culture might be like. Formal, rigid, and a "tight ship" administration is immediately evident. Social work practitioners adhere closely to agency policy as no deviations are likely to be tolerated. Rules are institutionalized, operating manuals are highly developed, and all agency personnel are held strictly accountable for social service outcomes. In-service training is minimal and centered mainly on task rather than treatment considerations. This means that emphasis is placed on how well the workers understand rules and policies rather than on the direct casework knowledge needed by the workers. They are more likely to have to secure the latter "on their own." Innovative notions about effective social services are discouraged and individuals who try new ideas are viewed as somewhat suspect. Outside consultation is either looked down on or made to fit pre-arranged agency plans. Reliance on social psychological thought and analysis is frowned upon.

Under these conditions, caseworkers are likely to become disenchanted with their professional world. Relationships with peers and with other social workers in the community may decline. You stick by the rules even in the face of apparent injustice. You become unwilling to take risks. Not taking chances in a profession like social work causes you to see everything in black and white. Clients do not look forward to working with you and avoid the agency whenever possible.

Many of you have experienced to some degree what has been described and the conditions noted surely influence the type of social work services that can be rendered. If you are a 9,9-oriented social worker, and find yourself employed in a 9,1-oriented agency, what would you do? The incompatibility might be destructive to your casework style. Could you render sound casework service to Mrs. Blair in a 9,1 agency? That would be extremely difficult. You might succeed until caught by agency regulations. You might even go into your backup style and become 9,1 yourself, succumbing to agency expectations. Unfortunately, the phenomena that often occurs is that caseworkers adopt a 1,1-oriented posture as a way of adjusting to the dilemma of a contradiction between what they feel is sound and what is demanded of them.

No matter what happens, your casework is affected by the agency's personality. It may even be accurate to say that your casework can only be as good as your agency permits it to be. If true, this suggests that caseworkers should seek to understand how to bring about change in their agencies in order to make them better places for social work.

Client Reactions

Clients react in numerous ways to a 9,1-oriented social worker.

Agreement with the Solution

When the caseworker tells the client to do something with which the client happens to agree, things go well. Doing what he or she thinks best makes the client feel good. The caseworker feels strong because it appears the client is complying. In fact, however, the client's thinking happens to coincide with the caseworker's.

Some clients "give" their problems to the caseworker to solve and feel a sense of relief at no longer being responsible. This reaction fits in with the caseworker's need to be strong but is only likely to make the client weaker and less capable of dealing with new problems in the future. The client has learned that "giving up" brings help from others. This relief from problems can create a positive attitude of love by the client for the caseworker who has taken the burden off the client.

Resentful Compliance

The client may privately disagree with the caseworker, but outwardly says yes and accepts the caseworker's counsel, even though his or her needs might not be met. If the client does what the caseworker wants but the problem remains unsolved, the client is likely to feel resentment. The caseworker is told by the client "I did what you told me but it didn't work." Because he or she is acting under instructions without real understanding or commitment, the client is limited to obedience without any gut-level enthusiasm for making the caseworker's ideas work.

Withdrawal into 1,1

Sometimes a client is resentful because the caseworker arbitrarily makes decisions for the client. The caseworker continues to act this way, constantly angering the client. A solution for the client is to retreat into a 1,1 orientation. When this happens, clients withdraw into indifference and are likely to change only in the most minimal way. The 9,1-oriented caseworker concludes something like "They are all alike, what can you do?"

Hiding and Forgetting

Another way for clients to escape the anger of a 9,1-oriented caseworker when expectations of the caseworker or agency are not met is simply to hide. Forgetting to keep an appointment or forgetting some part of an incident are mental tricks which relieve the client of tensions experienced toward the caseworker. This is repression at work, and it disrupts whatever communication the caseworker has achieved thus far with the client.

Fighting Back

In some instances clients react with open hostility, even resorting to threats or physically striking the caseworker. Complaints or accusations in the newspaper may follow. Open warfare turns the situation of conflict into a battle. The client may even succeed in getting the caseworker fired.

"Boomerang" Effect

There is one circumstance in which the boomerang effect of the client being dealt with in a 9,1-oriented way may provide a positive outcome. This can occur when the client is offended to such an extent that he or she is determined to solve the problem without help. Even though the outcome is constructive, this is certainly a poor reason to justify 9,1-oriented behavior, and it is difficult to identify other positive outcomes.

Childhood Origins

Childhood origins of Grid-based behavior are important to social workers and students for several reasons. First, early childhood behavioral patterns have always been important to caseworkers engaged in various casework settings such as medical, psychiatric, correctional, educational, and other similar social service enterprises. Social work literature and research devotes serious attention to children and to the dynamics of growing up. Second, because a cause and effect relationship exists between childhood origins and Grid-related behavior, the caseworker can gain greater insight into the client by understanding those antecedents that influence present problems being experienced by the client. Third, a grasp of childhood beginnings of Grid-oriented behavior helps the caseworker understand his or her own way of "coming on" to others, especially clients, in the casework interaction.

Where do Grid styles come from? It appears that certain ways of child rearing have predictable consequences for the Grid-related behavior of the child as he or she becomes a teenager and an adult.[2] This hypothesis has led to research, and clinical evidence now indicates that specific patterns of child rearing have had particular effects in terms of predisposing a child in the direction of one Grid style over another.

A sixteen-year-old boy appears before the juvenile court and is judged delinquent because of his involvement in several auto thefts. Although this is his first offense, the situation is serious and the judge wants to deal with the problem in a realistic fashion. Should the youngster be placed on probation? Should he be committed to a state training school? Should he be placed outside the home in some manner? The answer to such questions depends on the quality of the boy's relationship to his

---

[2]One of the richest analyses of parent influences on children and how these in turn emerge as adult styles appears in Horney, K. *The Neurotic Personality of Our Time.* New York: W. W. Norton & Co., 1937, p. 170.

How parents stimulate a child's motivations to dread failure is discussed by Missildine, W. H. and L. Galton, *Your Inner Conflicts — How to Solve Them.* New York: Simon & Schuster, 1974, pp. 196-201.

Parent behavior may become a model to the child for how he should treat others. This is discussed by Horney, K., op. cit., p. 87.

That child misbehavior can produce additional punishment and additional punishment promotes more misbehavior as a reaction of rebelliousness is analyzed by Missildine, W. H. and L. Galton, op. cit., pp. 171-174.

There is general agreement that punitive 9,1-oriented parents produce hostile and aggressive children who can also be punitive on a "like begets like" basis. See Missildine, W. H. *Your Inner Child of the Past.* New York: Simon & Schuster, 1963, pp. 204-209; Missildine, W. H. and L. Galton, op. cit., pp. 38-39; and Bell, G. D. *The Achievers.* Chapel Hill, N. C.: Preston-Hill, Inc., 1973, pp. 41-43.

parents. Can they manage him, or is he beyond their influence?

The judge expects reasonably accurate responses to such questions from the caseworker who will supervise the boy. The reliability of those responses is often dependent on how well the caseworker understands what has happened between the parents and the child.

Several different approaches to child rearing seem important in forming a 9,1-oriented child.

Like Begets Like

From the outset, 9,1-oriented parents tend to concentrate their child's attention on performance and achievement. Demands for performance may originate in parental guilt feelings. Parents see anything except hard work as frivolous. These guilt feelings are relieved when they see their child accomplish something through hard work. Though parents rarely show approval of what he or she does, the child learns to avoid punishment through compliance. Outright disobedience is punished physically or mentally through withholding privileges, ridicule, sarcasm, and so on. These undermine a child's self-worth and the child begins to see him or herself as a failure. Later, the child begins to treat others as he or she was treated. A vicious cycle develops in which the child cannot win. Because a child is expected to try even though he or she can only lose, winning, success, and strength take on an exaggerated significance. Winning in this sense is approximately the same as learning strategies of domination, control, and mastery over others. The best prediction is that punitive 9,1-oriented parents create 9,1-oriented children who are hostile and aggressive.

Paternalism

Under paternalism, parental pressure for achievement is specific in detail as to what a child may or may not do, just as in the case of 9,1-oriented child rearing. Even though the child may feel resentment, he or she complies, not so much to avoid disapproval as to secure approval. When parents give affection and approval in exchange for compliance, the child is likely to desire to meet parental wishes for performance. In this way a child learns the importance of being competent, of winning, and of excelling over others through a closely guided growth experience.

Unexpressed resentment, anger, and hate toward the parents result from excessive parental control, which rarely permits the child to express frustration because of the threat of loss of parental love. This resentment may persist into adulthood and often appears in the form of excessive anger, sometimes converted into hate for others such as clients who are too "weak" to deal with their own problems.

Incomplete Pampering

Pampering parents are submissive to the child's desires and seek to respond by giving the child whatever is desired. Then the parent-child relationship is turned upside down. The child becomes boss and the parents' adoration inflates the child's feelings of significance. Whenever parents fall short of being indulgent, the child learns to increase his or her demands to bring whatever is wanted. The pattern is set. The child becomes more demanding, more insistent, more given to tantrums. Demanding, in other words, becomes the means for learn to control and master parents. Once learned, the child applies the formula to others. This is a dramatic way of exercising will. Consideration for the rights of others becomes difficult for individuals who have become self-centered.

Childhood Deprivation

Being deprived in childhood may also stimulate the emergence of a 9,1 orientation in adult life. When a child feels psychologically or physically "abandoned," he may seek parental attention through "acting out" kinds of behavior. Parents label this behavior as "bad" and the child comes to see him- or herself in that same way. If this behavior is curbed, it can produce a 9,1-oriented adolescent who is angry and frustrated from earlier rejection and who comes to rely on achievement to compensate for earlier feelings of badness. Deprived children may also equate deprivation with evidence that they are weak and seek to get ahead at all costs to self or others in order to compensate.

No matter what parental attitudes toward child rearing lead to a child's learning a 9,1 orientation, feelings of anger are a universal reaction for an individual who has learned to live by a 9,1-oriented approach whenever mastery and domination motives are threatened. This anger is readily expressed by taking it out on others.

Implications of 9,1-Oriented Casework

While 9,1-oriented practices can yield productive outcomes in terms of final solutions for client's problems, the likelihood is that outcomes realized are at the expense of helping the client develop the necessary skills for dealing with similar problems in the future. Think back and recall instances when you were treated in a 9,1 way. No doubt you had feelings of frustration, rebellion, anger, etc. It seems reasonable that clients would experience similar feelings in a 9,1-oriented caseworker context. These are usually not favorable conditions under which to promote enthusiasm for change. Resistance is the more likely result. The client may even be led to sabotage your efforts as described earlier.

This prescriptive approach to intervention, though, does have a place. It is when the client has reached the point of impasse, hopelessness, or despair, and yet action is imperative to avoid further negative consequences. It is necessary for the caseworker to step into this powerless situation and insert the needed will to initiate the resumption of problem solving. When the client has renewed hope, the caseworker can relinquish full responsibility. The pertinence of prescription under these circumstances has to be looked at in a different light. It reflects a high degree of concern for the client. Prescription can be a 9,9 intervention in this special case if it represents the caseworker's readiness to substitute his or her will in order to help a client who has temporarily lost this capacity. Alternatively, prescription can take the form of a 9,1 intervention if it becomes an imposition of will in order to enforce the caseworker's point of view in a particular situation.

Consider what goes on among personnel in an agency when they are being treated in 9,1-oriented ways by dogmatic administrators or supervisors. Usually the coffee room talk or the hallway chatter indicates how the staff really feels about 9,1 conditions in the organization. If social workers themselves feel these destructive emotions, it is apparent that a client must experience the same kinds of feelings with his or her caseworker.

Even if 9,1-oriented practices help solve an immediate problem, the change will more than likely not be permanent. If behavioral change is promoted via compliance, the caseworker must be prepared to exert surveillance over the client to ensure that the behavior "sticks." This has never been a primary social work objective; even if it were, surveillance is hard to sustain. Caseloads are usually too large to permit a close watch over everyone. What this amounts to is that a client is not going to obey unless you can watch him or her. Of course, your capacity to exercise surveillance will never be as great as your client's capacity for doing what he or she prefers to do.

This leads us to an important point which social workers should keep in mind. Aronson reports that when people want privacy, they are probably not going to do what they are told. The greater the privacy, the less the compliance.[3] Client privacy is a traditional "social worker" value.[4] If you believe in things like client confidentiality, it is going to be very difficult to induce change through 9,1 methods.

Other psychologists have found that individuals are more likely to conform when there are group pressures to do so,[5] or when they have low self-esteem.[6] However, casework is an individual treatment process where group influence is minimal. Also, you are not inclined to do anything in casework that might cause more loss of client self-esteem.

---

[3]Aronson, E. *The Social Animal.* San Francisco: W. H. Freeman Co., 1972, p. 17.

[4]Biestek, F. P. *The Casework Relationship.* Chicago: Loyola University Press, 1957.

[5]Asch, S. "Studies of Independence and Conformity: A Minority." *Psychological Monographs,* 70, No. 9 (1956).

[6]Goldberg, S. and A. Lubin, "Influence as a Function of Perceived Judgment Error." *Human Relations,* 11 (1958) pp. 275-281.

There is another point to be considered when 9,1-oriented casework is your choice. The client will perceive you as authoritarian. If you find yourself utilizing a 9,1 style as a dominant approach, you might want to ask yourself "Why?" People do not paint a flattering profile of those who demonstrate authoritarian characteristics. Adorno and associates found that authoritarian personalities are preoccupied with ideas of toughness, conventionalism, superstition, stereotyping, destructiveness, and fear of sexual activities.[7] If it turns out that you basically have an authoritarian personality, these kinds of ideas will influence your casework service and cause your client's reaction to be less favorable than if you employed a style with fewer negative side effects.[8]

Where does this leave us? There are several ways of thinking about a 9,1 orientation. First, it is fast and efficient. It gets to brass tacks without wasting time. It cuts through to whatever the caseworker thinks is the central problem to be solved.

Against the advantage of speed and directness, as well as the utility of a prescriptive intervention for a situation of client hopelessness and resignation, there are certain significant limitations. The most important is that 9,1 violates important considerations of dignity, respect, mutuality, openness, and collaboration, attitudes essential for increasing the likelihood that basic problems will find resolution through a collaborative effort. A second implication is whether the client in fact will comply with the solution presented by the caseworker. Unless the client essentially agrees with the solution, he or she may give surface obedience to what the caseworker suggests or recommends, while at the same time holding private reservations. Under these conditions, the client is less likely to carry out the recommended solution, and his or her rebellion may go underground.

Even where the client complies, difficulties may build up for the future. By his or her compliance, a client is effectively

---

[7]Brown, R. *Social Psychology*. New York: Free Press, 1965.

[8]Leaders exercising coercive power (9,1) are found less attractive than those using other methods of influence. See Zander, A. and T. Curtis, "Effects of Social Power on Aspiration Setting and Striving." *Journal of Abnormal Social Psychology*, 64, No. 1 (1962) pp. 63-74.

saying "Tell me what to do and I will obediently carry out your instructions." This is not helping a client develop autonomy and the motivation for exercising it that is so essential for people to become mature members of society. Rather, it has the opposite effect of creating the circumstances under which the client returns when the next problem arises, saying "Tell me what to do." When the third problem arises, the client returns, again asking the caseworker for a solution to his or her problems. In summary, when the client resists a 9,1-oriented caseworker, the relationship between them is likely to become polarized, and it is unlikely that the intervention will have cycle-breaking effects. To the degree that a client complies, some change may come about, but when dependence occurs, it is likely that only a specific cycle may be shifted, as contrasted with more fundamental change in the client's approach to problems.

Does this mean that a 9,1 orientation has no place in your agency? From our standpoint, it means that a 9,1 orientation is less preferable than a 9,9 orientation, for reasons that will be elaborated on when we examine the 9,9 way of carrying out casework. However, in the real world it may be that the recalcitrance of the client, or the lack of skill of the caseworker, or the pressures on him or her by agency personnel, may deny him or her the time and the development opportunities essential for increasing the strength and effectiveness of the caseworker approach. In this sense, 9,1 may be the best under the circumstances, even though it leaves much to be desired in comparison with alternative possibilities.

Chapter 4

1,9-ORIENTED SOCIAL WORKERS

THE 1,9-oriented social worker is low on problem solving and high on concern for the client. When you engage in 1,9-oriented casework, you are extremely sensitive to the client, preferring to emphasize emotions and feelings over cognitive or behavioral outcomes. How the client "feels" assumes greater value than what the client "does." This client-centered change is designed to help individuals accept themselves as a means of finding their place in society.[1] When this is accomplished, the client is "free" to grow and to receive the social worker's help.

Motivational Dynamics

When relationships are accepting, the caseworker feels emotionally secure, and this is an expression of a positive 1,9 motivation. Because of this desire to be liked, the social worker is likely to be excessively attentive to what the client says. The caseworker seeks client approval by being very interested in the client, being kind and considerate, and above all, being responsive to client wishes and desires. When clients are pleased and reflect this in their friendly reactions, the caseworker feels a oneness with the client. For these reasons he or she cultivates an atmosphere of warmth. The word "deferential" catches a significant aspect of the basic attitude. The social worker who fears disapproval feels that it is "better to be safe than sorry," using ingratiating behavior to increase the likelihood of client approval.

The other side of the 1,9-oriented motivation is fear of disapproval. Fear is an intense emotional reaction, and fear of being personally rejected is one of the strongest. A 1,9-oriented social worker reacts to others according to built-in self-uncertainties

[1]Hall, C. S. and G. Lindzey, *Theories of Personality*. New York: John Wiley and Sons, 1957, pp. 475-476.

rather than according to the objective properties of the situation itself. In an effort to avoid rejection, the social worker is likely to be solicitous, acquiescent, and malleable. The 1,9-oriented case worker avoids imposing his or her will on others, saying "I would rather lead the client than push" or "I find out what the client thinks is okay and help it come true. People should be helped not goaded." This is 1,9 supportive casework.

A caseworker with a 1,9 orientation may, in fact, work hard, but does so to gain acceptance as contrasted with doing so because of interest in client problem solving or genuine concern.

Here is an example of a 1,9 orientation in casework.

SCENE: Caseworker's office in a large mental health center. A forty-four-year-old woman, Mrs. Marshall, comes to the center because she has been feeling very nervous, tired, and depressed.

SOCIAL WORKER: I'm sorry that you have been feeling this way, but now we are here to help you.

MRS. MARSHALL: I sure hope so, thank you.

SOCIAL WORKER: How long have you been having these feelings of nervousness?

MRS. MARSHALL: Well, it started about three months ago when my mother moved in with me after her stroke.

SOCIAL WORKER: Tell me more about your feelings on this.

MRS. MARSHALL: Well, my mother is an invalid. She is eighty-two and the doctor says she may not respond to anything. I work all day at a department store and then come home and take care of her.

SOCIAL WORKER: What about your husband?

MRS. MARSHALL: I have been divorced two years but that is another story.

SOCIAL WORKER: It seems that quite a lot has happened to you. It is important for you to talk about these things with someone who understands.

MRS MARSHALL: Yes, it is. I just feel so fatigued.

SOCIAL WORKER: I can surely understand that but I want you to feel free to tell me about all of the things that are happening to you. The important thing is you and how we can help you cope with the anguish you are now feeling. I would like for you to come in at least once a week, or more if you wish. Once we are able to discuss your feelings openly, you will begin to feel better and some of these problems will not look so bad for you.

MRS. MARSHALL: I hope my mother gets better.

SOCIAL WORKER: Tell me about how things were between you and her when you were growing up.

MRS. MARSHALL: Well, we had some problems; she was very strict and didn't want me to marry when I did.

SOCIAL WORKER: Some mothers are very protective; I'm sure she must have loved you very much. Perhaps you can tell me more about how things were for you at that time and maybe you would also like to discuss your relationship with your ex-husband.

This excerpt tells us something about how 1,9-oriented caseworkers practice. The primary concern of this caseworker is to explore the feelings of the client and to offer her the opportunity to talk. No mention is made about the real problems she may have in taking care of her invalid mother and working all day at the department store. Whether Mrs. Marshall really has too many demands on her time or not, attention is focused on her emotional state. The caseworker's main concern is that Mrs. Marshall commit herself openly and easily to discussing her full range of feelings about her life. The frame of reference employed is that Mrs. Marshall needs highly individualized casework in a warm, responsive, nonjudgmental milieu designed to give her psychological support. If Mrs. Marshall gains the freedom to grow, she is presumably better equipped to deal with her nervousness and her mother. Thus the caseworker might see her once a week for about three months, during which time Mrs. Marshall would probably begin to feel better about herself. If Mrs. Marshall does not receive this, she will be viewed as being on the brink of serious psychiatric illness.

Social Worker Behaviors

When asked to describe responsibilities, a 1,9-oriented caseworker may use the same words as one operating under any other style: to plan, organize, direct, and control the caseload. However, how these responsibilities are discharged is distinctive.

PLANNING: "I invite ideas from my clients and convey my confidences by saying 'I'm sure you will know how to do this and things will go well.'"

ORGANIZING: "Clients know pretty well what needs to be done. I'm ready to listen and offer help only if they need my suggestions."

DIRECTING: "I see my clients frequently and encourage them to come in whenever they wish. My desire is to help them secure the things they need once these needs become clear. That's the way to show people you are thinking of them."

CONTROLLING: "I rarely need to check on my clients because they try their best. I congratulate their efforts whether they are successful or not. Our interviews usually end by talking about why we did as well as we did and how we can do even better."

When the social worker utilizes a 1,9 orientation with a client, the casework dynamics assume their own special character.

Focus

1,9-oriented caseworkers focus very clearly on the client as an individual, oftentimes too much, tending to concentrate so much on the client that needed advice and counsel are withheld and important environmental or situational constraints are overlooked.

In Mrs. Marshall's case it can be noted that emphasis was placed on how she, as an individual, felt about her mother and about the emotional problems posed by the dilemma. When Mrs. Marshall stated that her problem seemed to start when her mother moved in, the caseworker said, "Tell me more about your feelings on this." When Mrs. Marshall wearily expressed hope that her mother would "get better," the worker reacted by asking how things were when Mrs. Marshall was "growing up." As Mrs. Marshall pointed to some problems in growing up, the caseworker quickly reassured her of her mother's love. The caseworker did not explore certain situational matters that could have been investigated in a constructive way as part of the casework process. For instance, the nature of the mother's stroke was not examined. Nursing home prospects, home maker services, Medicare, and Social Security angles were left unexplored.

1,9-oriented caseworkers focus consistently and with much concern on their counselees. One of the pioneering client-centered therapy advocates is Carl Rogers, whose work many readers know well. He says that successful client-centered therapy allows a social worker to enter into an intensely personal relationship with the client. The caseworker creates an environment in which the client can regain a sense of self-identity. Both caseworker and client can feel comfortable in this relationship even though neither party is aware of its eventual outcome.[2]

In social work literature, Biestek has captured this focus when he says —

> The relationship is the soul of casework. It is a spirit which vivifies the interviews and the processes of study, diagnosis, and treatment, making them a constructive, warmly human experience. It makes casework a practical living out of a true democracy's philosophy of the dignity and worth of the individual person.[3]

These are "pure" views of a 1,9 orientation that some social work practitioners find congenial as the basis for the practice of casework via client focus. The key intervention is an acceptance one. If you are a 1,9-oriented worker with Mrs. Marshall, you concentrate your efforts on soothing her feelings, listening, and talking. You are eager to help but the steps of change remain her responsibility. If Mrs. Marshall can be helped to "feel better," a new burst of energy may flow and she will be able to handle her mother's illness and her own disenchantment with renewed vigor.

The 1,9-oriented casework focus locates this behavioral change *inside* of the client as a person. Important as this support is, some more pragmatic help-giving avenues, like nursing home care and financial eligibility prospects that might have

---

[2]Rogers, C. *Counseling and Psychotherapy*. New York: Houghton Mifflin, 1942.

[3]Biestek, F. P. *The Casework Relationship*. Chicago: Loyola University Press, 1957, pp. 134-135.

contributed to solving Mrs. Marshall's problem, were left unattended. Think of it this way. If you needed sound medical, legal, or financial help in your life, would you go to someone you liked and made you happy, or would you go to someone you believed really knew their business?

Power Uses

Change under 1,9 conditions requires a minimal power differential between caseworker and client. If you proceed along client-centered lines you will tip the power balance toward your client, believing that the client is the master of his or her own fate and capable of making decisions without restricting demands by the caseworker. In effect, you reduce your own power in the casework process in order to center responsibility for change on the client. You avoid influencing the occurrence or direction of change beyond the point of "freeing" the client to grow. Surveillance is objectionable because it conveys a lack of trust. Trust and appreciation are central to your relationship, and conformity to preestablished expectations is contrary to this.

Social workers have been among the leading contributors to the literature on interviewing. There seems to be a consistent 1,9 pattern in what these social workers write on the subject. Interviewers are encouraged to be descriptive and to avoid being judgmental or evaluative in a good-bad, right-wrong sense. If a boy tells you that he cursed his mother, you might respond with "How do you feel about having responded that way?" If a woman tells you that her husband hit her, you would probably say "That must be very upsetting." The idea is to project awareness, interest, and acceptance on your part but not to pass judgment. Evaluation by the caseworker implies acceptance or rejection of the client from a position of authority over the client.

Consider Rogers' opinion, "Therapy and authority cannot be coexistent in the same relationship"[4]; from a social work classic, "Obviously the casework approach indicated here is suitable only in mild forms of delinquency . . . True delin-

---

[4]Rogers, C. *Counseling and Psychotherapy*. New York: Houghton Mifflin, 1942, p. 109.

quency often needs restraint and authoritative coercion."[5] Here we have a paradoxical 1,9 approach to power uses in casework treatment: (1) it is impossible or (2) it is possible only sometimes. In any event, 1,9-oriented social workers are not comfortable when using their power.

In the matter of Mrs. Marshall, the caseworker chose to focus on the client's feelings and did not attempt to probe into other areas. Mrs. Marshall was encouraged to talk about whatever *she* wished concerning her past relationships. While a more directive "push" by the social worker into task areas like Medicare might have yielded alternative ways to help the family situation, the "push" is something 1,9-oriented workers prefer not to do.

If you are a 1,9-oriented caseworker, you probably see your power coming from your ability to give love and consolation to your clients. If you choose not to use economic power, this leaves you only with the reward you offer as a supportive person. While this is a powerful influence, it has many drawbacks. The main limitation is that "love is not enough" because many clients have lost the will to initiate, or they may wish to do so but do not know how. If you shift into the role of instructor or guide, you run the risk of violating the client's expectations, because when power is exercised in these ways, it may lead to conflict.

We know that 1,9-oriented caseworkers dread conflict because it threatens warmth and approval, the main staples in the 1,9 emotional diet. This is what makes conflict seem so devastating. If conflict arises, the 1,9-oriented caseworker tries to get back into a close supportive relationship as soon as possible. If this fails, the worker may lose all personal influence.

Let us suppose that Mr. Jones, the sixty-six-year-old black man discussed in Chapter 3, came into the agency seeking emergency housing assistance from a 1,9-oriented worker. The worker suggests a housing project and Mr. Jones reacts with great anger again:

> MR. JONES: All you social workers are alike, right away you think that I should go into a housing project. No white man

---

[5]Hamilton, G. *Theory and Practice of Social Case Work.* New York: Columbia University Press, 1940, p. 233.

ever understood a black man anyway. I don't want a housing project and I think your idea is lousy.

SOCIAL WORKER: Mr. Jones, I am deeply sorry that I offended you with my suggestion. I certainly don't know what is best for you. You must be feeling very upset and embarrassed. This will not happen between us again. Tell me what it is you want once more.

The social worker's first reaction is to say, "I'm sorry," an appropriate comment. Note, however, the rest of the worker's commentary. "Tell me what it is you want" is another way of giving power to Mr. Jones by letting him go first. One way to stay in agreement and to avoid conflict is initially to listen to Mr. Jones' formulation of a solution. Rejection is more likely to result from the social worker expressing his or her own thoughts first. One reason is that whoever initiates a proposal is subject to criticism if the proposal is challenged. To a 1,9-oriented social worker, criticism of a proposal is a first cousin to rejection.

"I certainly don't know what is best for you" is another way of disclaiming responsibility for a solution to Mr. Jones' problem and, therefore, of averting trouble. "You must be feeling very upset and embarrassed" helps to explain and smooth over negative emotions that have arisen and to relieve the 1,9-oriented caseworker from feelings of personal rejection. "This will not happen between us again" is in the nature of profuse apology and is promising to take a back seat in the relationship. These kinds of responses are examples of how 1,9-oriented social workers avoid conflict and retreat from it by totally and permanently giving up responsibility for helping in a direct way to solve the client's problem.

This attitude of flight from conflict is typical of other and similar situations encountered by 1,9-oriented caseworkers.

Dependence

One of the valued qualities held by 1,9-oriented caseworkers is that they be consistent in applying the principle of self-determination, which is often the first thing taught in schools of social work. Client-centered caseworkers consistently and repeatedly encourage clients to make their own decisions and to assume responsibility. Social work prizes this client-centered casework approach very highly. This position is difficult for social workers to reject because clients so often seem to need love and encouragement more than anything else. The client-centered casework style means that clients must do all their own decision making.

Strictly speaking, clients are not permitted to lean on you or to become dependent on you. They are fully autonomous and your respect for them as free individuals requires you to support them as they make their own choices. You may reject concerns you have about client conformity to strict problem-solving guidelines, since implicit in those concerns are a host of subjective values and judgments regarding "correct behavior." We think that a 1,9-oriented worker would, indeed, have little regard for the importance of client conformity to expectations from societal or environmental requirements about solving client problems, because whatever the client decides is probably best for him or her.

There is another way to view this matter of self-determination. The dilemma is that while self-determination is valued, the client may be incapable of exercising it. The inability to do so may be from physical or mental health difficulties, financial problems, or family strife. What does the 1,9-oriented social worker do under these circumstances? Is decision making by the client continually supported, or, if not, should the principle of consistency be violated by the social worker becoming directly involved in the solution to the problem? Think about this and try to imagine yourself not involved in making direct decisions for your client.

There is a paradox in the dependency question. The 1,9 view constitutes a reaction to the culturally older 9,1 view. It represents social work's abhorrance of the notion that man is pleasure seeking or inherently lazy and indifferent. Attached to this is the idea that clients can be helped by caseworkers to sort out their disturbed emotions and feelings in order to know what to do. In Mrs. Marshall's case, she obviously needs someone who can help her ventilate her feelings. You may end up emphasizing her reactions to these feelings in the real world without intending to do so and without grappling with her real-life problems.

The result is that 1,9-oriented caseworkers may end up saying that the client "needs help." In some instances they may have to "take over" and make all of the decisions; then the client does not know what to expect. If there is inconsistency in this approach, 1,9-oriented caseworkers may have to pay the price of sometimes appearing uneven to the client when direct intervention is imperative to "save" the client from catastrophe.

Interviewing and Recording

These items receive top priority from 1,9-oriented social work practitioners but with a special twist added. Interviewing and recording must be *diagnostic* of feelings in order to have any real meaning.

Interviewers are encouraged to cultivate empathy (acknowledge to Mrs. Marshall that she must feel very tired), to communicate understanding (give her a tissue if she seems to want to cry), to listen to her voice (is it slow and hesitant?), to listen to silence (does silence increase tension?), etc. These and other dynamics are characteristic of 1,9-based interviewing and recording.

When you are recording information as a 1,9-oriented caseworker, it is not enough to interpret, analyze, and summarize your data briefly. There are two other requirements: the process between you and your client is also described; and the recording is arranged chronologically to show "growth." This means you spend a great deal of time capturing client emotions, reactions, and gestures and picturing your own feelings as well. Mrs. Marshall might be described this way:

> 3/3/77
>
> Mrs. Marshall, a forty-four-year-old woman came to the office wearing a black and gray dress and appearing very tense. She fingered the buttons on her blouse and seated herself very rigidly to the left of my desk. My compassion for her was aroused as she looked down at the floor a lot and seemed unable to concentrate on our verbal exchanges. She appeared to be tired, listless, and in need of sleep. At times she seemed

remote and reluctant to discuss her feelings about her mother's illness. Generally, she gave me the impression of a person with chronic depression, etc., someone who will benefit from a supportive relationship as she develops a solution to her problems.

1,9-oriented social workers record in this manner all the time, so to speak, and rarely settle for less than an emotionally enriched understanding of what they see and feel. The color of Mrs. Marshall's dress has special meaning. Seating herself to the left of the desk receives close attention. Mrs. Marshall is not simply tired but also listless, in need of sleep, remote, and reluctant to talk. The second, third, and fourth recordings tend to be as complete, or more so, than the first. Detailed differences in each recording are compared, and diagnostic statements sprinkle the entire record. These records are discussed regularly with supervisors and used to further understanding of the client. If you are a practicing caseworker, you may see some of this 1,9 orientation in your own approach to patients. If you are a social work student, you may recognize how important this type of coaching with respect to interviewing and recording is in your practicum or field instruction experience. How well students interpret these accounts is important to how positive their commendations will be from their practicum instructors.

Agency Personality

Agencies that tend to be informal organizations where continual dialogue is held between administrators, supervisors, and staff express a 1,9 orientation. Many learning opportunities such as case staffing, expert consultation, and external workshops are provided. A high level of personal autonomy exists and practitioners are encouraged to "do your own thing." Thus you are free to innovate, to spend long periods of time with clients, and to advocate sympathetically in their behalf. Therefore, if you are committed to a 1,9-oriented style of practice, in order to reduce the likelihood of tensions between your style and the agency personality, it seems almost mandatory that you work in a 1,9-type agency.

A 1,9 orientation spread throughout an agency produces an easy-going, country club atmosphere where people do what they enjoy at their own pace and with whom they like. Agency administration may even encourage this ambience because the director sees staff as his or her most important asset. Everything is done to see that the staff is satisfied with working conditions and with the director. Ensuring that people can fit into any situation with comfort, friendliness, and security is the 1,9-oriented administrator's desire.

Client Reactions

Client reactions to 1,9-oriented caseworkers range from feeling safe and secure within a warm and friendly atmosphere to feeling smothered, stifled, unchallenged, patronized, and wanting to escape from it.

Security

Where casework interactions reinforce a person's desire for approval and diminish the fear of rejection, the client may find the 1,9 atmosphere supportive and helpful. When asked about his or her attitudes toward a 1,9-oriented social worker, a client says "I like my social worker. I would not want anyone else." This client identifies with the worker because 1,9-oriented social workers listen with great interest and patience.

When the client/worker relationship is a clinical one, a client's security may be enhanced by what might be called "counter therapy." This condition occurs when the client or patient gets "hooked" on therapy so that it becomes a "hobby" to that person. The client learns therapeutic lingo, reads all the popular therapies avidly, and almost hates to solve the problem lest the opportunity of therapy goes away. This client may even begin to see him- or herself as a social worker.

Resentment and Frustration

Many clients are stimulated when confronted by their caseworkers. When such clients are not challenged, frustration arises if they feel their time is being wasted. An example of this occurs when clients react angrily to 1,9-oriented caseworkers who "won't answer my question." This causes resentment in clients who see the clinically based 1,9-oriented worker using therapeutic listening without rendering direct answers needed for seeing the real situation. By giving approval without providing opportunity for genuine accomplishment, a 1,9-oriented caseworker may provoke frustration among clients. This reaction is most likely when a 1,9-oriented social worker is dealing with a 9,1-oriented client.

Stifled Creativity

Clients who are committed to getting things done often see different and better ways of getting results. This might unsettle the 1,9-oriented social worker, and disagreements result. Clients served in a 1,9 way learn to withhold creative or original ideas about problem solving rather than putting them out only to see them smothered. The social worker interactions become dull and unrewarding to these clients, and change is retarded.

Problem Solving

When the true blockage to clear thinking is intense or confused emotions, this social worker approach can aid a client to become more objective. Under these conditions, reducing tensions associated with blocked emotions frees a client to tackle the "real" problem in a strong and effective manner. This is the situation where an acceptant approach with the client is most likely to have sound results.

Childhood Origins

1,9-oriented children become 1,9-oriented adults as the result of their interactions with parents and other adults. These interactions follow certain lines.

Paternalism

A 1,9-oriented child is reared by paternalistic parents to do their bidding in return for love and affection. This seems to happen most frequently when one or both parents analyze the child so well that they become expert in every detail of what the child is thinking or feeling. Thus, the parents exercise control over the child, telling him or her what to do, how to think, and what to feel, all in a way that makes the child dependent and appreciative of parental love and help. Each small step of advice and guidance is easy for the child to follow and accept with the result that autonomy is relinquished and love preserved.

Warmth and affection are extended to the child as approval of his or her dependence on the parents for direction. The parents' constant helpfulness unwittingly communicates to the child the danger of self-reliance, the importance of ensuring continued help through dependence on them for advice and support, and the warmth and approval that leaning on parents brings.

Under these conditions of rearing, a child learns to be responsive to all adults in order to gain their acceptance, love, and approval. The child has learned to ask "What must I do to gain adult approval?" or "How must I think or feel?" Thus, the child does whatever gains approval, not what promotes self-reliance and independence.

By comparison, when a child thinks and acts independently or spontaneously, parents may feel threatened. They communicate this to the child, saying something like "If you loved me you wouldn't do that." This stimulates the child's fear of rejection and inhibits the development of a desire to act autonomously. Parents who give love and affection in return for dependence are creating the conditions of a 1,9 orientation. Punishment that might promote hostility or anger is likely to be absent. The closest thing to it is apt to be parents' withholding affection.

Parents of a 1,9-oriented child are, therefore, paternalistic in their approach to child rearing. They exercise strong direction and control, not in a telling or demanding task-oriented way, but in the sense of undermining the child's confidence and independence. These parents say things like "Let me do it for you," "You're so nice," and "You always do what's right." The child learns to fear new, strange, and unfamiliar situations. Life is secure under the umbrella of loving parents, teachers, bosses, and others.

1,9-oriented casework is a continuation of the same attitude, though now the caseworker seeks love and approval from clients, finding the client-centered therapy approach a congenial way of avoiding conflict and stimulating love and appreciation.

9,1-Oriented Rejecting Parents

A second but probably less frequent childhood origin of 1,9 attitudes is from 9,1-oriented parents who reject their child to an excessive degree. Feeling rebuffed, the child develops stronger and stronger needs for approval, which go unfulfilled. Starved for love, the child seems to have an insatiable desire for affection. Any sign of rejection causes hurt and pain, and he or she reinforces efforts to gain approval, testing each new relationship for what is wanted most: love and approval.

Implications of 1,9-Oriented Casework

Many social workers find 1,9-oriented casework styles very appealing in the business of helping people. Many social work practitioners choose this approach because it is so congenial to their social work values. Person-centered methods also receive wide use in other helping professions. A 1,9 orientation places greater emphasis on the psychodynamics of individual changes than on the social determinants of behavior, something in which many social workers believe.

We would like to caution you about some built-in problems you can anticipate when utilizing 1,9-oriented casework.

Since 1,9 casework emphasizes the client as a person, you might easily be seen as permissive. Have you ever felt that you were a "soft touch" for your clients? If so, this can be a short distance from your getting "conned." In other words, you are creating conditions that encourage some clients to manipulate you — not an altogether desirable situation, expecially if you are dealing with a client whose interpersonal styles have been in this tradition. While there is no evidence that Mrs. Marshall is manipulative, the caseworker could readily have encouraged this trait by stressing present and past feelings so much. There were several specific things which Mrs. Marshall could have performed in a task-oriented manner for her mother. A manipulating client can avoid discharging such responsibilities by maneuvering the caseworker into discussing emotional issues. If this happens the worker ends up trading problem solving for 1,9 "caring."

1,9-oriented caseworkers also have problems with how clients perceive them. If your client thinks he or she has been talking to a wall for two months, he might explode with "Would you please stop answering my questions with a question!" 1,9-oriented social workers see this reaction as a therapeutic breakthrough because the client has admitted "hostility" or the inability to "trust" others. Unless you are an accomplished therapist, these interpretations of what could be ordinary behavior may cause you to seem insincere. It is difficult to be certain of another person's motives and reasons for behavior, and it may be unnecessary when solutions to problems are being found through joint effort.

Other problems associated with 1,9-oriented casework may cause you difficulties. Successful 1,9 change strategies require long-term treatment procedures. Because of its heavy psychological emphasis, you may find that helping your client takes a very long time as you develop your way through intricate interviews and prolonged diagnostic record keeping. Psychiatrists speak in terms of patients who require 3000 hours of therapy as an example of long-term reconstitution of a person's psychological makeup. When translated into 1,9-oriented goals you can expect that this too will consume extended time periods. While few people quarrel with the idea of "taking all the time you need" for the client, this does pose serious dilemmas in crowded public agencies with large caseloads. Thus, a 1,9-oriented acceptant intervention posture with respect to cycle breaking may take such an extended period of time that it is impractical to utilize it in terms of the benefits gained. 1,9-

oriented casework may be seen by outsiders as a sort of "luxury" service, which is not so affordable economically and not necessary if the client's real problem is manageable within the limits of the situation itself by changing that situation.

Additionally, 1,9-oriented social work puts you into a medical model view of your client and emphasizes the notion that the client is sick. This perspective has received serious challenges from writers who question the concept of mental illness,[6] the reliability of psychiatric methodology,[7] and the results of psychotherapy.[8] If you are committed to 1,9-oriented casework, you owe it to yourself and to your clients to investigate the issues raised by these writers.

In addition, a 1,9-oriented caseworker must have what Martin described as a tolerant personality.[9] This means that you are very trusting of others, secure, humanistic, empathic, and fair at all times. Tolerant 1,9-oriented caseworkers stress the practical over the theoretical and are committed to attitudes of mutuality, collaboration, brotherhood, and love. This list of desirable qualities is hard to acquire and has also been known to clash with the sometimes harsh, frustrated, and less benevolent culture patterns from which clients may emerge.

Finally, in an agency based on 1,9-oriented social work, how is that agency "accountable" to the community? 1,9 outcomes tend to be abstract. "Feeling better," "gaining identity," and "acquiring self-understanding" are complicated qualities to measure, and 1,9-based agencies find it difficult to demonstrate what they have accomplished. If an agency is perceived as being run by "a bunch of impractical idealists" it is less likely to receive consistent community support. There have been cases where agencies have indeed lost their respect because they were unable to account for their operational results. The noble motives of 1,9-oriented programs contained the seeds of their own deterioration.

Do these limitations mean that a 1,9 orientation has no place in casework? A 1,9 orientation is limited to the degree that it

---

[6]Szasz, T. *Law, Liberty, and Psychiatry*. New York: MacMillan Co., 1963.

[7]Glasser, W. *Reality Therapy*. New York: Harper and Row, 1964.

[8]Kiev, A. *Magic, Faith, and Healing*. New York: Free Press of Glencoe, 1964.

[9]Martin, J. G. *The Tolerant Personality*. Detroit: Wayne State University Press, 1964.

satisfies the needs of the caseworker rather than meeting the problem-solving needs of the client. This is not to say that a listening, supportive, encouragement-giving approach is inappropriate under all circumstances. This only means that it is inappropriate when the problem confronting the client is causing an emotional reaction rather than the emotional reaction being the cause of the problem. A 1,9-oriented caseworker is likely to confuse these two. A further point needs to be introduced, however, by saying that a listening, supportive, encouragement-giving approach, when essential for aiding a client to sort out emotions in order to be able to get rid of a problem, as we shall see later, is in fact a 9,9 rather than a 1,9 orientation. In the 9,9-oriented caseworker, it is the essential productive orientation for helping the client grapple with an emotional problem and in this way to facilitate the solution of operational problems.

Chapter 5

1,1-ORIENTED SOCIAL WORKERS

A 1,1-ORIENTED caseworker is characterized by low interest in solving the problem at hand and low interest in the client as a person. A social worker who has adopted this kind of an approach wants to remain with the agency but not to be personally involved in the real-life problems of its clients. This is likely to result in the caseworker going through the motions of interviewing clients, documenting discussions, complying with agency rules, and so on, but of having little more than incidental impact on solving client problems.

Motivational Dynamics

Though the social worker has emotionally resigned and retreated into indifference,[1] the positive motivation is to stay in the system. This means doing enough to preserve his or her job and to build seniority, but without trying to make a contribution that might really benefit clients, colleagues, or the agency. Staying in the system is facilitated by interest in documentation of every detail that might be contested and results in the caseworker being subject to question regarding competence. With all detail in order, there is little room for criticism. This caseworker expects little and gives little.

On the negative side, the caseworker's motivation is to "hold on" and avoid sinking into hopelessness and despair. Although feeling bored, drifting, and listless, the caseworker avoids

[1]Strategies of isolation are discussed in Argyris, C. "Human Relations in a Bank." *Harvard Business Review*, Sept.-Oct. (1954) pp. 63-72; and Lawrence, P. R., J. C. Bailey, R. L. Katz, J. A. Seiler, C. D. Orth, J. V. Clark, L. B. Barnes, and A. N. Turner, *Organizational Behavior and Administration: Cases, Concepts, and Research Findings.* Homewood, Ill.: Dorsey, 1961, pp. 237-238.

For factors in minimum communication see Hurwitz, J. I., A. F. Zander, and B. Hymovitch, "Some Effects of Power on the Relations Among Group Members." In D. Cartwright and A. Zander (Eds.) *Group Dynamics: Research and Theory.* Evanston, Ill.: Row, Peterson, 1953, pp. 483-492; and Kelley, H. H. "Communication in Experimentally Created Hierarchies." *Human Relations,* 4 (1951) pp. 39-56.

acting in ways that might expose him or her to dismissal. The 1,1-oriented caseworker avoids exercising initiative, either on behalf of the agency or the client. The reason is that initiative exposes one's actions to examination and potential repudiation. The safer way is to remain passive and "out of it," particularly if this can be done without appearing truly uninvolved. This results in a passive "take it or leave it" kind of attitude, where the "take" is whatever is the agency's minimum help to a client, and the "leave it" is "You make up your own mind." The worker is prepared to put up with the situation and to go through treadmills day after day.

The basic attitude of 1,1-oriented casework is exemplified in the episode that follows.

SCENE: Mrs. Muñoz, age 69, comes in to apply to the Food Stamp Office. She lives with her sister Anna, 67. Both took care of their aged mother who died four years ago. Mrs. Muñoz receives $235 in social security monthly and both sisters live on this. Anna has been chronically ill.

SOCIAL WORKER: How many members are there in your household?

MRS. MUÑOZ: Me and my sister Anna.

SOCIAL WORKER: How much income enters your home?

MRS. MUÑOZ: Only my social security.

SOCIAL WORKER: Did you bring proof of this?

MRS. MUÑOZ: Yes, I have this uncashed check.

SOCIAL WORKER: Thank you. Does your sister have any income or resources?

MRS. MUÑOZ: She has no income — only the house we live in.

SOCIAL WORKER: How much are your monthly payments?

MRS. MUÑOZ: The house is paid for.

SOCIAL WORKER: How much is it worth?

MRS. MUÑOZ: $16,000.

SOCIAL WORKER: Do you have proof of this?

MRS. MUÑOZ: Well, you can call Miss Garcia at the loan company and she can tell you.

SOCIAL WORKER: I'm sorry, but we need written proof for the files.

MRS. MUÑOZ: Maybe I can catch a bus and go get a letter and bring it back to you this afternoon.

SOCIAL WORKER: I'm sorry, but I do not have any openings

until 4:15 tomorrow afternoon, so let's just get some more information now. I see you have high medical bills; have you been sick?

MRS. MUÑOZ: No, my sister Anna is, and she has no income. The doctor has been kind enough to let me pay monthly.

SOCIAL WORKER: I see you have prescriptions. Do you have proof for these medicine payments?

MRS. MUÑOZ: Well, the drug store has never given me any receipts.

SOCIAL WORKER: I need to check this with my supervisor — excuse me.

This interchange gives some flavor of the dynamics involved in 1,1-oriented casework. The caseworker emerges as a sort of "custodian" of food stamps and this suggests a custodial approach to the client's needs. Custodial strategies are not really change efforts but reflect the caseworker's unique perception of his or her own role for staying "clean" in the system rather than a concern for inducing change that improves the client's life.[2]

Social Worker Behaviors

A 1,1-oriented caseworker avoids suggesting things the client might do and avoids taking a negative attitude toward whatever the client may want to do. This is more abdication than helping, as is shown in the following ways the caseworker might view responsibilities.

Planning. "I give broad suggestions only if it is necessary, and avoid specifying particular goals whenever possible. Each client does it on his or her own."

Organizing. "When left alone, clients do what is possible as they know their strengths and weaknesses better than anyone else."

Directing. "I carry the message to clients about what is expected of them by the agency. I pass the message on through the proper channels with as little interpretation as

[2]Further discussion of 1,1 dynamics is found in Riesman, D., N. Glazer, and R. Denney, *The Lonely Crowd.* Garden City, New York: Doubleday, 1950, p. 144.

possible."

Controlling. "I make the rounds with my caseload but I take little action on-the-spot if I can avoid it. Clients like it that way and I do too."

The 1,1-oriented caseworker avoids interfering, not for the reason that clients need the opportunity to learn from their own efforts, but out of a lack of involvement. Thus a 1,1-oriented caseworker occupies the position in only a superficial way, passing like a shadow over the ground, leaving no permanent mark on the agency or on clients. Neither the agency nor the clients leave their mark on the 1,1-oriented social worker who is seen but not heard and operates on the basis of neutrality and camouflaged involvement.

Focus

For all practical purposes, the 1,1-oriented caseworker is unfocused. If any focus is present, it reflects the mechanical aspects of casework; namely, specifying information about limitations on the client or what may happen if the client does not conform. The frame of reference is basically uncentered.

This uncentered approach represents a way of staying in the agency without being really interested in clients or their problems. Caseworkers have pressures to effect client changes on one hand and resistance from clients on the other; thus, they often experience failure. The result is an increasing conviction that the client's tendencies toward having problems become greater than any caseworker's efforts to be helpful. Eventually a 1,1 orientation causes caseworkers to rationalize that the client's maladaptive behaviors are too deeply ingrained for real change to occur. If change does transpire, it just happens or comes about from unanticipated circumstances because of the client rather than from caseworker attempts to help. The 1,1-oriented caseworker becomes a passive observer of what is happening with the client. The caseworker monitors the situation, with a goal of doing the minimum, regardless of whether this may or may not help the client.

The interview with Mrs. Muñoz exemplifies this. The caseworker asked questions in a routine manner but most of them were designed to produce straight data. The worker did secure accurate information. Period! The caseworker insisted on detailed documentation but did not react to Mrs. Muñoz' more emotional cues like "Anna has been chronically ill" or "Anna has no income."

Power Uses

The only source of power tapped by 1,1-oriented caseworkers is that which comes from their official *position*. When they find it necessary to assert power, they rely on the official authority vested by law, ordinance, or agency policy. They merely quote the rules or the manual, and that takes care of the problem! No exceptions are made. The 1,1-oriented social worker becomes very uncomfortable and immobilized if there is no rule on the issue or the remedy is not spelled out clearly.

As with social workers operating according to other Grid styles, the 1,1-oriented caseworker also is faced with pressures, dissatisfactions, and unhappy or resentful clients who call upon him or her to act in their behalf. The 1,1-oriented caseworker's reactions to such situations range from pseudo compliance, through neutrality, to physical withdrawal from the situation. This keeps him or her relatively free of involvement and conflict. This is called the "ostrich dynamic." Keeping his or her head buried, the 1,1-oriented caseworker does not have to face problems and other disagreeable situations.

One way to avoid conflict is to be seen and not heard. 1,1-oriented workers seldom participate spontaneously in discussions and do not reveal their thoughts unless asked for them, and even then the tendency is to be vague, abstract, or noncommittal. By not saying anything meaningful to the client, the social worker avoids being provocative and does not have to explain or defend personal points of view. If all the social worker gives the client is silence, then it is easy for him or her to conclude that the worker agrees with what the client is doing. If someone asks "How are things going?" the answer is "Okay." Further discussion is not encouraged by this kind of answer, yet there is nothing negative about a nice, bland *okay*, particularly when it is not followed up with "How are things with you?" Commenting objectively might start an argument, and arguing is a drag. If X and Y are said to follow Z, well, okay.

When a client or even a colleague in the agency complains about something, the 1,1-oriented caseworker either ignores it or implies that the displeasure has been noted. The response is likely to be, "It'll probably work itself out" or "More time is needed to think things over." An example follows.

If Mr. Jones, the elderly black man discussed earlier, says:

> MR. JONES: All you social workers are alike. No white man ever understood a black person. I think your idea is lousy.
>
> SOCIAL WORKER: People have always had problems understanding each other. It's not easy. But, if you wish any help from me, I can only offer suggestions within the limits of what I have to offer. Perhaps this is not enough, but it is important for you to make up your mind. There are other people who might snap at the chance we are offering you.

1,1-oriented caseworkers use power to initiate and maintain logistical routines about record keeping and literal interpretations of the rules. Mr. Jones needs to find out how he fits into what the agency says can be done in order to qualify. If he does not, it is of no concern to the caseworker. Power channeled toward accomplishing these ends is noticeable to clients and the social worker is likely to end up appearing rather laissez-faire. The caseworker becomes a detached onlooker who enforces purely impartial regulations. This unimaginative, mechanistic casework approach stamps him or her as a red-tape artist.

Dependence

A 1,1-oriented caseworker who does not become closely enough involved with the client to stir up any feelings is unlikely to arouse dependency reactions. This is seen in the case of Mrs. Muñoz. The caseworker made no effort to assist her with transportation to the loan company, to secure a financial statement, or to check with the pharmacy about unpaid prescriptions. This would have required effort from the caseworker when in fact Mrs. Muñoz could do this herself. Thus, the client may rely on the caseworker to receive what he or she has coming but will not seek assistance on emotional issues, nor will the client expect help in prevention aspects by anticipating problems down the road that can be avoided.

A 1,1-oriented social worker tends to view the client as somewhat irresponsible but also sees the client as having arrived there independently. This caseworker has seen many persons like Mrs. Muñoz over the years and has become discouraged about just how much change can be accomplished with these kinds of clients. She is seen as a free person who is good or bad as a matter of genetic chance, impossible circumstances, or because "that's the way it is." The 1,1-oriented caseworker therefore might see Mrs. Muñoz as reaping the fruits of her own activities and as a person from whom real change cannot be expected.

The 1,1-oriented caseworker is likely to be fast and efficient. More people like Mrs. Muñoz are disqualified for food stamps by this worker than by anyone else in the agency. The reason, of course, is that the caseworker avoids being taken to task for wrong judgments by not exercising judgments that can be easily challenged.

Interviewing and Recording

This area is of great importance to 1,1-oriented caseworkers. A 1,1-oriented caseworker comes across as a cool character with twelve years of experience until one realizes that he or she has done this same thing for twelve years. Chronological recording is current and official. A 1,1-oriented caseworker is likely to keep the office neat and tidy. Records are maintained on a daily basis, and weekly evaluations are conducted on the status of all cases. Rationale is provided in great detail for all decisions even when there are no compelling questions involved. A 1,1-oriented caseworker prefers memos and letters to picking up the phone and "working a deal" for the client. Correspondence is always up to date.

Effective interviewing consists of securing quick, crisp, and pertinent information. It is in the interview that the officiousness of 1,1 becomes visible to the client, who concludes that he or she is "just another face" to the worker.

Securing clear information is important for the files, but in the case above, closer attention to Mrs. Muñoz' responses about her sister Anna might have yielded even more important possibilities. For example, would Anna qualify for Medicaid? In many instances, this could have covered her back medical bills, which are now burdening Mrs. Muñoz. The caseworker chose to focus on eligibility guidelines of the *agency* rather than zero in on the real needs of the client and her sister. If the caseworker had focused on real needs, what would have been more important: proof of social security income or knowledge about Anna's Medicaid or Medicare status?

Let us say that you are a graduate student in practicum and you are serving as the social worker in this situation. You know from your practice classes that it is vital to secure sound information and to record it properly. You know from social policy classes that certain major social welfare programs such as food stamps, social security, and Medicare have been developed to alleviate social problems. You know from human behavior and the social environment courses that Mrs. Muñoz is feeling great stress, perhaps even a pre-depressive condition, and you know something about the consequences of this condition for her.

How might you put this knowledge to use in your practice of social casework? There is a tendency among practitioners, for example, to emphasize the behavioral dynamics and to respond to Mrs. Muñoz' stress by utilizing a technique such as catharsis, or by trying to make a definite psychological diagnosis such as anxiety reaction. While these may very well prove pertinent, there are other, more likely, possibilities of your being helpful. For example, if you have substantial understanding of relevant social welfare programs and know how to connect your client with them, *that* might be the best treatment for her. A well-handled referral could become the most potent cure for Mrs. Muñoz' problem because it might result in swift economic relief, which would then neutralize her stress, regardless of your diagnostic assessment.

In your school experience you may encounter the notion that referrals can be made by "technicians" and that the social worker is needed for more "professional" matters, those complex psycho/social evaluations of clients. We think that sound "referral therapy" is no less important than diagnostic classification. We also think that incisive interviewing and recording aid the referral process.

Agency Personality

The dynamics of 1,1-oriented casework can be understood in the light of agency circumstances.[3] Often it is the agency that induces 1,1-oriented practices. If you are a casework practitioner, or a graduate student with previous agency experience, you may recall certain conditions under which you worked that promoted a 1,1-oriented organizational life.

One situation that is likely to bring on a 1,1 outlook in a caseworker is his or her failure to meet the demands of the agency and the resulting ostracism this may bring about. Some social service agencies set up grandiose goals for serving clients but they are unable to muster personnel with sufficient knowledge, skill, or resources to meet them. Failure results in caseworkers adopting a "why try" attitude and pulling back into indifference. Some federally backed social service projects might be placed in this category. Many times unclear goals, excessive paper work, or the division of work policies produce monotony and frustration. Have you ever felt that "the system" worked against your giving first class casework services?

What happens when, despite your good efforts, there is no promotion? These outcomes occur in social work agencies as they do in other organizations. A not uncommon response by social work practitioners to such conditions is to make a 1,1 adjustment. When professional staff development is neglected you tend to see lower levels of satisfaction, commitment, and responsibility along with higher levels of boredom.

The implications of this for individuals who seek help from such an agency are ominous if the goal is to provide change for

---

[3]Organization conditions promoting 1,1 are pictured in Argyris, C. *Personality and Organization.* New York: Harper, 1957, pp. 76-122; Mills, C. W. *The Sociological Imagination.* New York: Oxford University, 1959, pp. 165-176; Bensman, J. and B. Rosenberg, "The Meaning of Work in Bureaucratic Society." In M. P. Stein, A. J. Vidich, and D. Manning (Eds.) *Identity and Anxiety.* Glencoe, Ill.: Free Press, 1960, pp. 181-197.

those who seek your assistance. Organization theorists use the word *entropy* to describe organizational systems where growth and vitality have ceased and the agency runs down and reaches a "blah" stage. 1,1-oriented staff members contribute no input, and this absence of new ideas makes for a dull or regressive casework program. Entropy permeates the entire agency environment. Eventually, the agency may be abolished or put into a "holding pattern" which serves only the symbolic needs of people.

Client Reactions

Clients served in a 1,1-oriented way may go out on their own, searching for their own solutions, or themselves drift into 1,1-oriented reactions.

Clients Develop Their Own Solutions

Clients who know how to function on their own within a given agency may welcome a 1,1-oriented caseworker. When the client is self-initiating, the caseworker's withdrawal is almost unnoticeable. If Mrs. Muñoz had not been handicapped by age and ability to get around, she might easily have managed some help despite the 1,1-oriented rule-bound caseworker. Sometimes another client, or a politically knowledgeable person who knows the ways of local government, can advise a Mrs. Muñoz of "who to go see" and these contacts help her circumvent an inert caseworker.

This kind of a "get up and go" client reaction may come about as a result of frustration with a 1,1-oriented caseworker. The client, out of desperation, is "pushed" to act on his or her own resources, sometimes on an "I'll show you" basis. Then a good result occurs for bad reasons.

9,1 Reactions to Caseworkers

The 9,1-oriented client reaction may be to attack the caseworker by reporting him or her to a higher authority or to threaten legal redress when nothing happens or things go wrong.

Into 1,1

Another response is for the client to accept the circumstances as inevitable and move into a 1,1 corner, taking whatever services are available from a 1,1-oriented caseworker or an entropic agency on an "It's better than nothing" basis. Many caseworkers agree that some cases like that of Mrs. Muñoz occur. She goes away disqualified for food stamps; or in some instances she receives her food stamps, but she gains no further assistance because the 1,1-oriented caseworker will "let it go at that." When this happens the client is no longer "being helped to help him- or herself" according to this basic social work value. Tolerance for such 1,1-oriented client attitudes is built into many organizations, particularly where red tape prohibits innovative practices.

Leaving

A common response to being served in a 1,1 way is for the client to recognize the situation for what it is, even though this is unacceptable. A client may find him- or herself "dead-ended" by this kind of social service and simply leave. Clients who are members of "out" cultures or powerless minority members sometimes react in this way rather than by pushing a 1,1-oriented caseworker or agency for what they have legitimately come to expect.

Childhood Origins

There are various childhood origins of a 1,1-oriented Grid style.[4]

---

[4]Excessive punishment as a parental basis of child rearing is described in Missildine, W. H. *Your Inner Child of the Past.* New York: Simon & Schuster, 1963, pp. 121-122; and Missildine, W. H. and L. Galton, *Your Inner Conflicts - How to Solve Them.* New York: Simon & Schuster, 1974, pp. 120-121. A child's withdrawal as a means of reacting to coercive parental practices is described by Horney, K. *Neurosis and Human Growth.* New York: W. W. Norton & Co., 1950, p. 275.

Threat of desertion is a mechanism for controlling the child; see Branden, N.

→

9,1-Oriented Parents

A 1,1 orientation may be brought about by parents who maintain extremely close supervision or create an over-coercive situation involving constant criticism and rebuke. In either case, the child is left with little or no freedom for the development of initiative or personal discretion. Punishment is immediate and the child's will to resist or fight back is broken. His or her only option is to escape by withdrawal. The child satisfies family demands but protects him- or herself from its pressures on a "be seen but not heard" basis. This "teaches" a child to build a protective wall around him- or herself and make no more than survival adjustments.

A second child rearing pattern is where parents may simply be passive, not reacting to the child either in a punitive or loving way. When parents respond in this neutral manner over extended periods, the child is left alone, unstimulated to learn the skills that result from participation. When continued lack of social stimulation, coupled with parental neutrality, persists over time, the child begins to embrace behavior with a 1,1 flavor — withdrawal, indifference, uninvolvement, and inner emptiness.

Response to Deprivation

Another childhood origin of a 1,1 orientation is observed when a child is separated from his or her parents and placed in a hospital or other residential institution soon after birth. After

---

The Disowned Self. New York: Bantam, 1971, pp. 8-9.

A 1,1 orientation can be created during the first year of life when a child experiences nothing but an "emotional vacuum." Even though physically and nutritionally provided for, if the child remains untouched, uncarried, uncraddled, unsmiled at, unlaughed with, unplayed with, then it can be predicted that a nonresponse reaction comparable with apathy will emerge. The child becomes less able to make spontaneous, free, open contact with other children or with adults. This kind of child rearing, sometimes found in "sanitary" orphanages, has been verified in child research. It is the basis for some aspects of a 1,1 orientation in adults, who themselves may feel emotionally withdrawn, disinterested, and unable to gain interest or involvement in their child. See Spitz, R. A. and K. M. Wolf, "Anaclitic Depression: An Inquiry into the Genesis of Psychiatric Conditions of Early Childhood." *The Psychoanalytic Study of the Child,* 2 (1946) pp. 313-342.

an initial period the child becomes withdrawn and ceases to make demands, crying only occasionally, without observable cause. Eventually the despair is replaced by shallow reactions that hide a lack of responsiveness. These patterns of submitting to circumstances without commitment may be one of the important predisposing factors for a dominant or a backup 1,1 orientation among adults.

Withdrawal from Conflict

Still another set of circumstances fostering a 1,1 orientation is when parents are in deep conflict with one another. Children may "freeze" under these circumstances, immobilized by anguish. The only escape for the child from the intense emotions is total withdrawal. They come to react to any conflict situation in similar terms, sometimes to the point where it becomes a dominant 1,1 Grid style description.

Implications of 1,1-Oriented Casework

While a 1,1 orientation may result in a few problems getting solved, and while it is unlikely to cause great sparks of controversy for an agency or to bring about corrective action in supervising the 1,1-oriented individual caseworker, it is anything but what is needed to strengthen casework as a profession or to help a client in need of assistance. Most caseworkers agree that client problems do not go away if just left alone. There are a number of hazards for both caseworker and agency when concerns for both problem solving and the individual client are low.

The client reads you as being indifferent; it seems like you just do not care enough. You are merely doing a job. Second, you are seen as a caseworker who does not exercise judgment or take chances. Admirable as "not risking it" may be under some circumstances, it is positively disastrous when risk seems necessary and you hold back. Third, you never make a mistake if you are a "pure" 1,1-oriented caseworker. The worker took no risks by requiring complete proof at all times in the circumstance of Mrs. Muñoz. The social worker gave the impression of a person willing for the client to make a return trip to the agency but unwilling to venture an opinion without consulting the supervisor, who was unavailable at the time. This type of caseworker is judged as a rule enforcer and might even enjoy this reputation because it might be taken as showing that he or she is responsible. The cycle-breaking possibilities of a 1,1-oriented approach are likely to be quite limited. If a client appears who fits the requirements of a program by happenstance, then help is extended. If this assistance is useful, the cycle may be broken. Little or no responsibility is felt by the 1,1-oriented caseworker to bring about change.

Are these behaviors really assets for your agency's reputation? If change is a goal and if compassionate help-giving is your objective, then 1,1-oriented casework strategies are dead-end behaviors and should be avoided.

1,1-oriented practices cause your agency to be viewed with dismay by social workers in other community agencies. Referrals to your agency are not made with confidence. "I have to take my client over there myself in order to get results." 1,1-oriented organizations begin to get the reputation of being ritualistic. "It takes an act of Congress for them to accept a client," and the net outcome is bad public relations.

There is one other phenomenon that can lead to 1,1-oriented outcomes among individual caseworkers and for the agency alike. Some agencies become overspecialized. They lose sight of the whole client picture, and this adversely affects their policies and procedures. For example, an agency may narrow its services only to diagnostic or psychiatrically oriented cases even though it is expected to have more general functions. It can become over-selective in hiring practices, somewhat elitist, insisting on close diagnostic supervision of practitioners and spending nearly as much "professional time" discussing psychodynamics as it does rendering direct services. Caseworkers in this kind of an agency who are able to see the total situation of the client, beyond psychological considerations, tend to become disenchanted. The agency program fails to recognize problems that do not come within its stated interests, treating all nonpsychiatric matters with detachment.

When a 1,1-oriented caseworker rationalizes why he or she is less productive than others, as may be evidenced in a smaller caseload or in fewer closings, the blame is likely to be placed on something or someone else. For example, "The government and the bureaucracy have gotten too big." He or she may blame "the onslaught of technology for dehumanizing people," concluding "I want no part of this." This worker complains that the university or the school of social work "did not really prepare me for today's requirements." The social worker might be heard saying things like "The administrators of this agency don't really care about our needs" or "Society doesn't really want to help these clients" or "Social work will never amount to anything important" or "Who can really count on other social workers to do what needs to be done." Some observers have suggested that 1,1-oriented conditions are widespread, especially in large public agencies. A kind of anomie is fostered when social workers begin to lament the very system that pays them, and this double bind precipitates 1,1-oriented behaviors. These rationalizations serve the purpose of justifying passivity, indifference, and a "can't do" spirit and make it unnecessary for the social worker to admit that he or she is not involved.

Sociologists have described certain conditions that are, in some respects, similar to the 1,1 behavior described here. The word used to describe this is *anomie,* another way of characterizing the 1,1 adjustment. Anomie pictures that person who has no entity, who is rootless, drifting, and reveals no direction in his or her behavior. Under anomie, personal behavior has lost its aim except for bare subsistence. Students who have an opportunity to study the theory of anomie in some detail find that it has relevance to social problems like poor mental health, crime and delinquency, drug abuse, alienation, and so forth. Some students have considered seriously whether some degree of anomie does, indeed, exist in social work when large numbers of practitioners become "burned out." Other scholars have been known to express feelings that the very school of social work that trains them might itself be described as suffering from anomic conditions. They have witnessed faculty members who display little interest in students, whose teaching styles or content have become old or irrelevent, and who are either living off past laurels or have lost their enthusiasm for real-life social service experiences, growing out of an "ivory tower" effect.

We are not speaking about social work practitioners who sometimes (maybe on Friday afternoons) slip into discouragement over what seems to be the odds against their being effective. We think you are entitled to your moments of frustration because they are real. If too many social workers become too disenchanted too much of the time, the seeds of 1,1 "don't rock the boat" values are planted and germinate, blossoming into a full-blown 1,1-oriented agency where neither you nor the clients are well served.

Can you recognize yourself falling into the 1,1 trap? This is an important question if you wish to prevent that outcome. If you start feeling useless, thwarted at every turn, and begin to imagine there is no future in your agency, these thoughts may be indicators of 1,1 inclinations. If you find yourself using statements like "Who cares?" or "That's his problem" or "People don't appreciate what I do around here" or "It's up to them. There's only so much I can do" — or if you call in your supervisor too often, "passing the buck" upwards — you may be slipping into 1,1-oriented moods. We urge you to notice if that is happening to you and also whether other social workers are tending to behave in similar fashion.

Perhaps you will agree that we already have more 1,1-oriented practices in social casework than we need in this profession.

Chapter 6

5,5-ORIENTED SOCIAL WORKERS

A 5,5 CASEWORK orientation is revealed when an intermediate degree of concern for finding a solution to the client's problem is coupled with an intermediate degree of concern for the client as a person. The caseworker knows that "Rome was not built in a day" and therefore pursues a gradual, step-at-a-time kind of approach. He or she also knows that "You can lead a horse to water but you can't make him drink" and therefore seeks to offer encouragement to the client without demonstrating a deep commitment to helping the client resolve the dilemma.[1]

Motivational Dynamics

A social worker who is positively motivated by desire for belonging wants to be "in." Direction is sought through finding out what others think would be okay in order to respond in a like manner.[2] This leads to a tendency to be superfi-

---

[1]Several basic inquiries into the 5,5 orientation have appeared since World War II. These include Whyte, W. H. *The Organization Man*. New York: Simon and Schuster, 1956; Wheelis, A. *The Quest for Identity*. New York: W. W. Norton & Company, Inc., 1958; Riesman, D., N. Glazer, and R. Denney, *The Lonely Crowd*. Garden City, N. Y.: Doubleday & Co., Inc., 1953; Putney, S. and G. J. Putney, *The Adjusted American*. New York: Harper & Row, 1964; Harrington, A. *Life in the Crystal Palace*. New York: Alfred A. Knopf, 1959; and Kilpatrick, W. *Identity and Intimacy*. New York, N. Y.: Dell Publishing Co., Inc., 1975.

[2]Fromm speaks of the 5,5 approach as having a "market orientation," where the manager's aim is to sell himself successfully in the corporate managerial market. ". . . His sense of self does not stem from his activity as a loving and thinking individual, but from his socio-economic role. . . . His sense of value depends on his success: on whether he can sell himself favorably. . . . Human qualities like friendliness, courtesy, kindness, are transformed into commodities, into assets of the "personality package," conducive to a higher price on the personality market. . . . Clearly, his sense of his own value always depends on factors extraneous to himself, on the fickle judgment of the market, which decides about his value as it decides about the value of commodities. He, like all commodities that cannot be sold profitably on the market, is worthless as far as his exchange value is concerned, even though his use value may be considerable." (Fromm, E. *The Sane Society*. Greenwich, Conn.: Fawcett Publications, Inc., 1955, pp. 129-130.)

cial in convictions and to embrace the kinds of attitudes depicted above. This individual is cautious and takes cues as to what to do from others, such as clients, according to what they want. What others reject, the 5,5-oriented caseworker also rejects. The result is that this caseworker is unlikely to have deep ideological commitments, whether political, literary, social, humanistic, or otherwise. The caseworker feels much better when evaluated positively by clients or other social workers and is willing to sacrifice long-term gain for the client for short-term popularity. He or she will start and stop, twist and turn, shift and go, and yet seek to remain noncontroversial. The "best foot is put forward," even if this effort is not what the client really needs. A 5,5-oriented caseworker does almost anything to gain and keep attractiveness in the eyes of colleagues and clients.

Sometimes a 5,5-oriented caseworker is unsuccessful and feels out of step. This can lead to loss of membership status with others. Viewed from the negative side of his or her motivation, the caseworker wants to avoid looking bad and being outside the mainstream. Risking being put "out" by clients or colleagues results in anxiety, so the 5,5-oriented worker has difficulty in making anything other than routine decisions.

The concern for the client as a person and the concern for problem solving are brought in delicate balance, calculated to promote acceptance by the client in terms of how he or she perceives his or her own needs. This is based on the often realistic assumption that casework is a complex enterprise in which one cannot realize the best of both worlds but should attempt to secure as much as possible of both for the client without losing status in the eyes of supervisors and colleagues. These dynamics are illustrated in the following example of 5,5-oriented casework.

SCENE: Mike and Ann Ferguson come to a private agency for marital and sex casework. The therapists, Mary Stevens and Ted Haynes, are 5,5-oriented psychiatric caseworkers who are handling the Ferguson referral.

MARY: Mrs. Ferguson, I'm so glad you were able to bring Mr. Ferguson in to see us about that "little problem" because it's the type of thing that could cause you serious trouble in the future.

TED: Yeah, these sort of problems can get sticky, if you know what I mean. (Laughs)

ANN: Well, it took some convincing but here we are. What do we do now?

MARY: First of all, let's agree to call each other by our first names, if that's OK. I'm Mary and this is Ted, and you're Ann and Mike. We are going to get to know each other very well so let's not be formal with one another.

MIKE: I just don't know what good all this is going to do.

TED: Where there is a will there is a way. Why, I've had this problem myself on various occasions and I know it can be solved. Temporary impotency in men leads some women to feel guilty that maybe they caused it but we can work it out together. Just last year we had a very prominent politician in here and we got it straightened out in a month. I'll tell you one thing, he is taking much better care of the country right now. (Laughs)

ANN: I know that Mike has been very upset about this problem lately and that is why I was able to get him to come in but I'm not sure he will agree to stay.

MARY: Mike, our program usually takes about three months if you come in weekly, but if you agree to come in for one month we'll put everything we have into this and try to get some results by then. If you are not satisfied you can quit then. If you are satisfied we can then specify how long it will take. We want both of you to be completely satisfied.

TED: That's the way we operate and we think that we have been quite successful. We are both members of the National Sexual Psychotherapy Society and Mary will be regional chairperson of that society during this year. We want you to take this article we recently wrote for a journal in our field because the article will tell you something about what we believe. We also want to know what you believe.

MIKE: Sounds good.

TED: You betcha. Work with us and you will see what we mean.

This interaction describes the motivations and actions of a 5,5-oriented social worker whose primary desire is to belong. Being popular means putting together a package of qualities that will be sought after by others, in this case, Mr. and Mrs. Ferguson. 5,5-oriented social workers strive to become interesting and to make friends with the clients. Mary and Ted discuss "in" topics and make themselves status people — by reference to membership in the National Sexual Psychotherapy Society and demonstration of popularity as evidenced in "Mary will be regional chairperson . . . during this year." In this situation, Mr. and Mrs. Ferguson are going to be asked to "give and take" in order to solve their sexual problems and become well adjusted. Mary and Ted will serve as positive models, so the Fergusons can identify with them, i.e. become "like" them. For this to succeed, Mary and Ted must themselves project the image that they are "in" and therefore are positive examples to Mr. and Mrs. Ferguson.

Social Worker Behaviors

A 5,5 orientation to casework involves "responsive" leadership. Many ways of moving forward, always in step with what others expect, typify this approach. It stays well within the bounds of what other sex therapists are doing to help their clients as the criterion for appropriateness or pertinence. This amounts to a philosophy of "me-too-ism," where change is by copying or by improvisation, not by developing a goals-oriented direction or by experiment. The result is not chaotic nor is it coherent; it is eclectic.

According to this line of thinking, a social worker does not *command* or *direct* to get casework done so much as he or she *motivates* and *communicates*. Exerting formal authority is avoided. The approach is to request and to sell in order to get clients to want to change.

PLANNING. "I make my casework plans based on what I know my clients will accept while avoiding what they are likely to resist. In other words, I plan, but my plans consist of what each client will think is okay."

ORGANIZING. "I explain things to my clients and double-check to make sure they think what I request is in line with their expectations. I encourage them to feel free to check with me if they don't understand what to do."

DIRECTING. "I keep up with each client's performance and review his or her progress from time to time. If a client is having difficulty, I try to reduce pressure by rearranging or reducing expectations for the client's progress."

CONTROLLING. "I tend to emphasize good points and avoid appearing critical, though I do encourage clients to identify their own weak points for themselves. Clients know that I take their thoughts and feelings into account."

The caseworker sees it as very important to communicate, to elicit suggestions from clients, and to consider their points of view in the casework plans. The goal is to avoid "pushing" clients past the point of agreement. The 5,5-oriented social worker does not try a new idea until it has been tested by others or discussed with the client to see if he or she is ready to accept it.

The 5,5-oriented caseworker sees his or her optimal role to be that of a catalyst. Rather than pushing for one's own solution to the client's problem, the client is aided to identify needs, gather information, and in other ways supply procedural assistance. This enables the client to discover alternative solutions and to evaluate one possibility against another as to which is the better solution. In this way the client feels a sense of personal responsibility for the outcome while the caseworker aids the client without actually controlling him or her.

This description provides an indication of the 5,5-oriented way of dealing with what the caseworker regards as inherent contradictions between problem-solving and people needs. Neither set of needs is ignored. He or she scales down problem solving to what people are prepared to accept. Clients are encouraged to offer suggestions, which the caseworker then uses to either reduce the statement of results expected or to decrease pressure for results and thereby eliminate frustrations, as well as to show that he or she listens. This kind of compromise in problem solving that also avoids complete sacrifice of people needs is a balancing act. It involves giving up some of what one thinks is possible to get the other desired result, namely, pleasant collaborative clients. This orientation assumes that clients are practical and that they realize *some* effort must be exerted to change, even though the change may not be too great. This is the hallmark of a 5,5 approach. It does not seek the best solution for the client ("that would be too ideal") but a solution which finds acceptability, even if not truly sound.

Focus

When you practice 5,5-oriented casework you concentrate on the *relationship* between you and your client. Most approaches emphasize the quality of relationship but 5,5 adds a special dimension. The casework relationship must be *attractive* to the client; this is key. It is not just a "we" proposition between worker and client; it has to be a "beautiful," "neat," or an otherwise desirable liaison. By focusing on the development of such a relationship, 5,5-oriented caseworkers hope to secure a positive response to themselves as individual change agents who can then use this attractiveness to influence clients. Such focus does tend to create a personalized tie between you and your client. Your capacity for leadership is brought forward with public relations expertise so that clients like the Fergusons have a favorable reputation to emulate. The focus takes on a "fifty-fifty" quality designed to facilitate "give-and-take" procedures, which help you maintain your likeableness as a caseworker.

One of the most important characteristics of a 5,5-oriented practitioner is his or her image, without which attractiveness could not be maintained. When you "give and take" with the Fergusons such as "If you agree to come in for one month we'll put everything we have into this," you are bargaining to maintain your image. The Fergusons have no idea of what is involved but they would be very unappreciative to reject it out of hand. You hope the Fergusons will see that you really "understand." After all, you are married too. This "regular guy" approach is sometimes useful because you come out looking real. This can be a powerful medium through which change may be secured, particularly if the problem is superficial with the solution more or less ready to fall into place. In 5,5-oriented casework your energy goes into keeping an attractive relationship rather than really grappling with the problem to be solved.[3]

[3]Use of flattery, showing interest, and so on in order to gain influence over another is described by Carnegie, D. *How to Win Friends and Influence People.* New York: Simon and Schuster, 1964, p. 27.

Power Uses

The 5,5-oriented caseworker relies heavily on social power and on personal attractiveness in dealing with clients. He or she works hard to get their acceptance. In gaining the admiration of clients, the 5,5-oriented worker feels that cooperation can be won by virtue of the fact that those who admire the caseworker will desire his or her good favor and will conform with expectations in order to gain it. Therefore, as a 5,5-oriented caseworker, you are more than willing to share your power with the client. On a scale of 1 to 10 you would function at about 5 1/2 or 6, just enough to tip power in your favor but only enough so as not to be perceived as directive. This means you compromise, mediate, and make deals with your clients if these strategies preserve your attractiveness and the salience of the relationship.

The power variable shows up most clearly whenever conflict enters into 5,5-oriented casework activity. A 5,5-oriented caseworker responds to conflict by using power in several different ways. One is to fall back on tradition, long established agency practices, or routinized casework procedures.[4] When a caseworker can rely on history to support a point of view or recommended solution, he or she is relieved of being called to account for acting according to a personal conviction. Conflict related to the exercise of independent judgment is avoided.

In everyday usage, diplomacy and tact refer to other 5,5-oriented kinds of actions because they are calculated to reduce conflict by structuring the relationships of people and their interactions according to preset, even though often vague, "rules." Thus Mary Stevens tells the Fergusons "First of all let's agree to call each other by our first names" without determining if they are really comfortable with this or whether they believe in that kind of an informal approach. Protocol tells

---

[4]Reliance on tradition for conflict management is a hallmark of a 5,5 orientation. See Merei, F. "Group Leadership and Institutionalization." *Human Relations,* 2 (1949) pp. 23-39; Riesman, D., N. Glazer, and R. Denney, op. cit.; Beach, D. S. "An Organizational Problem — Subordinate-Superior Relations." *Advanced Management,* 25(12) (1960) pp. 12-15.

people what to do in the absence of their having internal commitment about what is sound.

When agency policies and regulations are ambiguous regarding the course of action to take, a 5,5-oriented social worker looks to supervisors and others for answers as a way to hide uncertainty. He or she may tactfully tease "guidance" out of a supervisor and thereby be seen as initiating responsibility without risking deviating from what the supervisor thinks best.

Another way of avoiding uncertainty and of reducing the likelihood of conflict is to deal with a problem at least partially in terms of the client's frame of reference about what the client feels as personal needs rather than from the caseworker's own professional perspective. The needs felt by Mr. or Mrs. Ferguson may be the real ones or they may be unrelated to the real problem. No matter. If you can help them solve their felt needs they are satisfied and you are appreciated. That is why Ted Haynes had to make sure to say to the Fergusons "We also want to know what you believe."

By invoking tentativeness, a 5,5-oriented worker can also defer using power and in this way avoid conflict. The reason stems from being cautious in order not to take a position that may turn out "wrong." From a 5,5 perspective it is seldom wise to confront conflict directly, even when the evidence is that confrontation may be the only way to bring resolution to the problem. Frequently it is possible to take some of the caseworker's ideas and some of the client's ideas and put them together. The compromise solution may not be perfect but it it likely to be bought. The true goal of casework competence is to achieve the best result in terms of problem solving for individual clients. The best is rarely defined by something which is in the middle, intermediate, or which represents a splitting of differences between divergent points of view, as in the case of the 5,5-oriented approach. Though the client's problem is relieved, the solution reached may leave deeper-lying problems unresolved.

Dependence

A 5,5-oriented approach encourages social equality between

you and your client. This leads to a hidden but split assumption on your part, to the effect that clients are "basically okay" but they need your leadership to bring it out. Clients need meaningful affiliations with persons they can rely on (again, as in the Ferguson's situation), and you emerge as this kind of person. This makes followers of the clients and places extra responsibility on you as an image-creating change agent.

You tend to see your clients as ready to change on the basis of their need for accepting relationships that, when used constructively, can become the source of motivation for more adaptive behavior. When Mr. Ferguson said "I just don't know what good all this will do," the caseworker responds with "Temporary impotency in men leads some women to feel guilty that maybe they caused it." This calls attention to the caseworker's insight and ability to neutralize such knotty problems. The caseworker attempts to gain the reputation for himself or herself as a technically capable helper, rather than concentrating on his or her client's real behavior per se. Accordingly, the caseworker feels that it is important to project and understand the problems of the client, while at the same time being mindful of the requirements of the problem as defined in a particular situation.

This social equality is what many clients think they require at certain points in their lives. When achieved with a sensitive, secure, and knowledgeable caseworker, this relationship can produce therapeutic results that enable the client to examine him- or herself in new ways. He or she is trustful of the caseworker and this releases psychic energy for solving client difficulties, but the goal to be reached tends to be set in such a way as to aid the client to feel progress is being made without really dealing with the basic problem.

Interviewing and Recording

The actions of 5,5-oriented practitioners in this regard are generally calculated to emphasize the importance of the client-worker relationship. Written information reflects a search for positive aspects in that relationship. Social worker assessments of client progress stress client responses to the caseworker as a person, how they have made advances together in problem solving, and how they have mutually identified new objectives to be pursued.

One word that describes 5,5-based casework interviews is the *sociability* and friendliness of the social worker. He or she is often "high" with optimism. "There is nothing we cannot accomplish together if we really want to." Interviews become fun sessions. Inviting your client to get a Coke and going out of your way to give him a ride home after the interview might be integral parts of a session. You are eager to meet your client at a hot dog stand or in a tavern or in a park, wherever "the action is." These all show the client you are an action person, an equalitarian, ready to do whatever is the "in" thing.

These overtures of informality can be well received, and 5,5-oriented caseworkers love to do these kinds of things. Many 5,5-oriented caseworkers are highly developed, well put together personalities, people who "fit" the "now" culture and feel no tension or stress in becoming equals with their clients.

Interviews are likely to be interspersed with vignettes or examples from your own life as a social worker and as a real person who has lived in the actual world. You tend to utilize examples of life heroes or of yourself as a person who has made it in the face of adversity and are worthy of client emulation. This can be an excellent technique, as the objective is to nourish those client contacts with you that stress your congeniality. This is shown by Ted Haynes telling the Fergusons that, "I've had this problem myself on various occasions and I know it can be solved."

Agency Personality

There is clear and widespread adherence to the idea of established authority. Executives and supervisors are "looked up to." This becomes a powerful managerial influence, because these administrators tend to be "status figures" who are tolerant and also interested in staff morale. A 5,5 kind of agency presents an environment that is favorable for client goodwill and feelings of acceptance. The agency can be thought of by the public as therapeutic, helpful, and reputable.

It is easy to describe a 5,5-oriented agency because it takes on various features characterized by appreciation of the agency bureaucracy through an informal atmosphere around division of labor as contrasted with strict accountability or a laissez-faire approach to responsibility. Staff members get along well and an air of "regular fellow" is discernible. Clients see friendly caseworkers, and the surroundings are homey.

A strong public relations program may be an important part of agency life. Staff members are heavily involved in community affairs and receive consistent and good media coverage. The agency's program enjoys a good image in the community and receives the support of prominent people.

Client Reactions

Because it is so apparently reasonable, clients rarely react against being served in 5,5-oriented ways in hostile or aggressive terms, or with disgust, or by leaving. They are far more likely to "get in step" and, though sometimes disappointed that things go slow, feel that progress is being made.

There is, however, a range of client reactions. They include the following.

Like Begets Like

The prospect, sometimes, is that under a 5,5 orientation clients begin to think and react in the same way as they are treated by the caseworker. Because actions are "reasonable," in the sense of being accommodating on a give-and-take basis, it may come about that caseworker and clients do move along in a steady-pace way. For example, although Mike Ferguson came in thinking he did not know "what good all this is going to do," when Ted finished telling him all about his and Mary's expertise (in a reputation-building way), Mike finished up by saying "Sounds good."

Status Game

Once immersed in a 5,5-oriented system, a caseworker may

enjoy the status game and work to refine the skills needed to stay within it, describing life and work in this fashion: "This is a great organization. It is interested in helping *people*. It provides me an opportunity to do what I want, which is to help others. I get along very well with staff and the agency really cares about its staff, so I will grow professionally and meet all my economic needs here."

This acceptance of a status quo concept of professional life, with its conventional values, status, and step-by-step progress through reasonableness, is a 5,5 response. It is an uncomplicated approach characterized by accommodation and adjustment. The caseworker's commitment demands no effort beyond staying up or maybe just a little ahead of the pack. As an example, Ted and Mary played a variation of the status game with the Fergusons by zeroing in on the prestige they enjoyed as members of the National Sexual Psychotherapy Society. The client's reactions usually are positive. Everything looks good even though there is no assurance that hard-core or "nitty-gritty" client problems are being addressed. The reasonableness of everything serves to obscure the real problems and no one, including the client, may realize this.

1,1 Drift

Some clients, however, may detect the 5,5 orientation, recognize that it is not getting to fundamentals, and still be unable to get the caseworker to respond to more substantial issues. If it turns out that Mike Ferguson does not get more realistic reactions from his therapists he may drift into a 1,1 orientation, accommodating his wife's desire for help, while expecting that "nothing" much will happen.

Statistical 5,5

A social worker may treat clients on the basis of an "everyone is different and unique" approach that gives everyone what they expect. This appreciates individual differences in comparison with the "everybody fits in" attitude of a straightforward 5,5 orientation but puts no one under any real challenge. This is the "statistical" 5,5-oriented worker who may employ all casework Grid styles, doing what is most "acceptable" with each client, whether or not this is producing change via problem solving. He or she operates all over the Grid by doing whatever the clients expect, and his or her casework style averages out to be 5,5.

The clients' reactions to this, if they even get a chance to compare, is to see the caseworker as inconsistent. Clients feel confused on how to relate to the caseworker, who thinks of him- or herself as "flexible," while the client may be thinking of the worker as "all things to all people." This "flexibility" is discussed in greater detail in Chapter 8.

Childhood Origins

Parents whose children come to embrace the 5,5 orientation as a dominant style are most likely to be 5,5-oriented themselves. They are guided by outer expectations more than by their own inner convictions. The social ethic of adjustment[5] based on appropriateness as defined by others places an ultimate value on being in step, and this is what they teach their children. This becomes their overriding source of direction in child rearing. They value a child who can fit into the appropriate group, take on popular points of view, who feels "in" and gains satisfaction from belonging. The child identifies, through his or her parents, with the values, rules, and morals of the community without really developing anything approaching an inner set of values.

At least two parental guidelines tell the specifics for child rearing efforts that lead to this kind of adjustment.

"Do What Others Do"

The child's attention is focused on getting along with other children in the same age group. Exaggerated emphasis is likely to be placed on the undesirability of being left out. The child is reminded repeatedly that "others will not like you if you are

---

[5]Adjustment and fitting in as a value in child rearing is discussed in Kovar, L. C. *Faces of the Adolescent Girl.* Englewood Cliffs, N. J.: Prentice-Hall, 1968.

different, but you will always have friends and be popular if you do as others do." This can have a strong anxiety-inducing effect and may increase a child's readiness to accept prevailing norms, which serves to reduce anxiety about his or her own acceptability. Happiness and virtue come to be equated with popularity, which is itself equated with conformity. Peers become dominant in molding a 5,5-oriented child's reactions. From a child's point of view, parents are likely to seem preoccupied with what other children do, so it appears that the child's generation knows best.

Emphasis on Image

The 5,5-oriented girl is concerned with how her mother looks and acts with her and her friends as opposed to how she thinks and feels about things, issues, and people. This social-centered and "rules-oriented" approach to child rearing does not result in strong relationships with parents, who are apt to praise the child for external attributes like being "pretty," "handsome," or having a "good voice" rather than to react to the child as a thinking, feeling, and striving person. The shallowness of the parent-child relationship leaves such a child few or no anchorages other than to be "in," to be popular, and to have status in the eyes of his or her peers.

Expert Model

Another source of child guidance is from whichever child development experts are in vogue at any particular point in time. The experts who give information about when motor skills appear and at what rate and in what sequences, when and how a child plays with other children, and when particular intellectual capacities can be anticipated to appear give 5,5-oriented parents a basis for building their expectations. When their child fits the model, parents feel secure.

Implications of 5,5-Oriented Casework

When as a caseworker you use a 5,5-oriented approach, you

may find yourself promoting behavioral change in your clients because this Grid style is potentially influential in several ways. The client likes you and is generally willing to try and please you in various ways because he or she knows you do "care." This type of casework can also become satisfying to you personally because it enhances your reputation and importance.

The major difficulty in a 5,5-oriented casework style is that it goes about social work through what is "tried and true." This means reliance on standard procedures and fixed routines of various sorts. The tendency is for the caseworker to adhere closely to agency policies and, when these are unstated, to use informal rules and what other caseworkers are doing with clients as a model for one's own work with clients.

The end effect is of many "solutions" that help the problem but that fail to solve it. The reason is that tried and true practices rarely get to the heart of the specific problem confronting Mr. and Mrs. Ferguson here and now. The caseworker can do something, but it is unlikely to bring the relief they need in order to move forward again under their own initiative.

Like other Grid styles, a 5,5 orientation is likely to be more successful if you are also aware of some built-in problems which come with it. Aronson[6] has identified some factors that tend to produce the attraction you require when relying on a 5,5 orientation, and these factors are not easily operationalized. For example, there are three personal attributes that seem to enhance your image: (1) you need to possess a high level of technical competence, (2) physical attractiveness can make a difference (but this is not totally necessary), and (3) similarities between you and the client may increase the possibilities of successful change. Secord and Beckman[7] suggest that if you like the client and the client likes you, a situation is created where "liking leads to liking." This also enhances the probability of client acceptance of your casework efforts.

We are sure you will agree that these qualities are all desirable and praiseworthy. Yet they also lead to a question: How

---

[6]Aronson, Elliot, *The Social Animal.* San Francisco: W. H. Freeman Co., 1972.

[7]Secord, P. and Beckman, C. "Interpersonal Congruency, Perceived Similarity, and Friendship." *Sociometry,* 27 (1964) pp. 111-127.

many caseworkers can be expected to have these qualities? It puts the practitioner in a delicate position if he or she wants to be a 5,5-oriented worker but does not possess these attributes in sufficient strength.

This leads us to a common result obtained by 5,5-oriented caseworkers. Given that you are attractive and that you are getting somewhere with your clients, what happens if your image loses appeal? Furthermore, as many of you know quite well, within the rules you may be called upon to make decisions and recommendations your client does not like. This might cause you to lose some or all of your positive qualities and make your relationship suddenly very tenuous. Add to this the possibility that a 5,5-oriented caseworker leaves the agency, and his or her successor, who has not established the same image, takes over the same caseload. What tends to happen to the caseload under these conditions? Because of variables like these, both the direction and duration of change become shaky and subject to numerous distracting influences. Moreover, change achieved on the basis of emulating a surface image is analogous to "cure by transfer" and tends to endure only so long as the caseworker is both attractive and near at hand.

Setting yourself up as a model for clients is potentially a very good approach, but we have already indicated what can happen if you lose your appeal. Many programs such as Alcoholics Anonymous, Convicts Anonymous, Ex-Addict Models, etc., are based on the attractiveness of the person who "knows" because he or she once had the problem. The results from this philosophy are not yet known. There are certain areas where the 5,5-oriented caseworker may be effective. They are often the ones who get clients to take the first step when fear is involved (such as convincing youth to register in school or to prepare for a G.E.D. test). They approach agency heads or other professionals with confidence. They are skilled in the catalytic role of offering procedural help for identifying needs, collecting information, and formulating and testing alternatives for solving problems. A 5,5-oriented caseworker is likely to be effective short-term in cycle-breaking situations where it is important to "get the client moving" quickly toward a solution.

In long-term cycle-breaking situations, a 5,5-oriented worker may have other problems too. He or she may be seen as "wishy-washy" and as being more concerned with "doing something rather than nothing" as compared with searching deeply for a sound solution, which may be much more difficult to attain. The "love at first sight" effect, which a client experiences with the 5,5-oriented social worker, drifts into disenchantment when the worker continues to try to maintain popularity at the expense of more "gutty" issues facing the client. Ted and Mary may be very attractive and also possess status in their specialty, but if they are not able to deal with the "rock bottom" problems faced by the Fergusons, neither of those qualities will make a difference. 5,5-oriented caseworkers are likely to maintain agency and self-prestige, but more often than not, reputation does not solve problems.

5,5-oriented practices cause your agency to be viewed as venerable but safe and worthy of support by community leaders. However, clients are likely to see them as having preset criteria for the kinds of problems they will or will not deal with, resulting in the client feeling that the agency is not really responsive to the real problems that people confront in daily living. In addition, 5,5-oriented agencies tend to become havens for the kind of social worker who is more concerned with the techniques of professionalism than with the finding of solutions to real-life problems; therefore, they are less likely to experiment with new or controversial approaches to the induction of change.

How does an agency come to be characterized by a 5,5 culture? One aspect is in hiring practices. Those most likely to be employed are social workers who qualify by standards set long ago, to which they continue to adhere, but which are not necessarily in line with current needs. In addition, agencies tend to become 5,5 in their orientation because they gear themselves toward providing what the conventional community expectations are rather than exercising leadership in bringing social work into fuller and more effective use. It may also be that private agencies tend more in a 5,5 orientation than do public institutions, because boards of trustees wish to see the agency adhere to conventional lines of practice from which little criticism is likely to result. Such agencies may break out of the characteristics that cause them to be 5,5 in their orientation because of community pressures of various sorts or the requirements of federal grants, etc.

Do you recognize yourself as embracing the 5,5 tried-and-true orientation of social work? If you tend to see yourself repeating the same techniques and pat formulas more or less without regard to genuine understanding of the client, this may suggest that you are slipping into a 5,5 mode of convenience. If you look to your supervisor for your rewards more than to the gratification that comes from seeing real client progress, this may also be an indication of moving into a 5,5 orientation. The final test might be this. Do you find yourself now rejecting innovations and experiments that, when you joined the agency, you thought were of significance to the richness and progress that social work might make? If you feel that you are in a 5,5 orientation, you may wish to reexamine your practices in the light of the chapter which follows.

Chapter 7

9,9-ORIENTED SOCIAL WORKERS

9,9 IS a theory of casework that couples a high concern for solving the problem at hand with a high concern for the client as a person. The 9,9 orientation might be called caring through contribution, as demonstrated in finding solutions to problems in active collaboration with the client.[1]

Motivational Dynamics

The positive motivation of a 9,9-oriented social worker stems from the desire to make a contribution to the client's successful solution of his or her problem coupled with a commitment to involve the client in the solution-seeking

[1]9,9-oriented concepts of involvement, participation, commitment, conflict resolution, etc. were brought to early definition by Simmel in 1908. See Simmel, G. *Conflict* (Trans. by K. H. Wolff). Glencoe, Ill.: Free Press, 1955; and Metcalf, H. C. and L. Urwick, *Dynamic Administration: The Collected Papers of Mary Parker Follett.* New York: Harper, 1940, pp. 31-32. The theory and concepts of 9,9 management find expression in the research of Lewin and associates in the 1930s, particularly the concepts of *participation, goal-setting, involvement* and *commitment, interpersonal relations,* and strategies for individual and organizational *change.* See Lewin, K. *Field Theory in Social Science.* New York: Harper, 1951. See also Lewin, K. "Forces Behind Food Habits and Methods of Change." *Bulletin of National Research Council,* 108 (1943) pp. 35-65; Lewin, K. "Frontiers in Group Dynamics: Concept, Method and Reality in Social Science: Social Equilibria and Social Change." In T. M. Newcomb, and E. L. Hartley (Eds.), *Readings in Social Psychology.* New York: Holt, 1947, pp. 330-344; Lewin, K. "Frontiers in Group Dynamics: II. Channels of Group Life: Social Planning and Action Research." *Human Relations,* 1 (1947) pp. 143-153; Lewin, K. *Resolving Social Conflicts: Selected Papers on Group Dynamics.* New York: Harper, 1948; and Lewin, K. "Behavior and Development as a Function of the Total Situation." In L. Carmichael (Ed.), *Manual of Child Psychology.* New York: Wiley, 1946, pp. 791-844. For a discussion of and additional relevant references to Lewin's work, see Deutsch, M. "Field Theory in Social Psychology." In G. Lindzey (Ed.), *Handbook of Social Psychology,* Vol. 1. Reading, Mass.: Addison-Wesley, 1954, pp. 181-222. Extensive documentation as to how various experts in different fields have dealt with issues related to 9,9 in comparison with other Grid styles are shown in the Appendix of this book.

process.[2] These values promote openness, spontaneity, and shared responsibility for accomplishing clear and sound goals. There is a sense of gratification, enthusiasm, and excitement from making a contribution.[3]

What a 9,9-oriented social worker seeks to avoid is selfishness, as evidenced in doing less for the client than the case deserves, and the sense of discouragement likely to result when less than a "total" effort fails to solve the problem.

If you are operating under 9,9 motivations, you see yourself as a partner in problem solving, acting in collaboration with clients when that is feasible, and acting for them when clients are unable to take collaborative steps in their own behalf.

The following depicts 9,9-oriented casework.

SCENE: The following interaction occurs in a family service agency rendering general social services to clients in various

---

[2]In examining the literature and experimental work concerned with participation, it is important to distinguish between pseudo and genuine participation. Attempts to make people think or feel their ideas are important, or manipulation of ego involvement, or artificial status-raising activities are not seen to be sound participation. The work of Coch and French and the insights of Levine and Butler make significant contributions to the 9,9 concept of participation. See Coch, L. and J. R. P. French, Jr. "Overcoming Resistance to Change." *Human Relations,* 1 (1948) pp. 512-532; and Levine, J. and J. Butler, "Lecture Versus Group Decision in Changing Behavior." *Journal of Applied Psychology,* 36 (1952) pp. 29-33. For additional representative experimental studies and discussions, see the work of Lewin, previously cited; and Marrow, A. J. and J. R. P. French, Jr. "Changing a Stereotype in Industry." *Journal of Social Issues,* 1, No. 3 (1945) pp. 33-37; Lewis, H. B. and M. Franklin, "An Experimental Study of the Role of the Ego in Work; II. The Significance of Task Orientation in Work." *Journal of Experimental Psychology,* 34 (1944) pp. 195-215.

[3]The motivation to make a contribution of a 9,9 character is explained by Fromm as an act of giving. "This experience of heightened vitality and potency fills me with joy. I experience myself as overflowing, spending, alive, hence as joyous. Giving is more joyous than receiving, not because it is a deprivation, but because in the act of giving lies the expression of my aliveness." Seen in this light, giving or making a contribution is a manifestation of self-actualization. See Fromm, E. *The Art of Loving.* London: Unwin Books, 1956, p. 26.

The emotional aspects of a 9,9-oriented relationship are seen as consisting of at least four components: care, responsibility, respect, and knowledge. Fromm, E. *The Sane Society.* Greenwich, Conn.: Fawcett Publications, 1955, p. 38.

Family and other analogies to the work situation are developed in Wolfe, D. M. "Power and Authority in the Family." In D. Cartwright (Ed.), *Studies in Social Power.* Ann Arbor: Institute for Social Research, 1959, pp. 100-101; Vroom, V. H. *Some Personality Determinants of the Effects of Participation.* Englewood Cliffs, N. J.: Prentice-Hall, 1960, pp. 1-18. Rollo May devotes Chapter 12, 287-325, to the meaning of care, equivalent to the motivational care of a 9,9 orientation; see May, R. *Love and Will.* New York: Norton, 1969.

situations of need. The client is Mr. Rodriguez and the caseworker is Mrs. Lee.

MR. RODRIGUEZ: I have a very serious problem and have no idea of how to solve it. We got word that my older brother, Theodore, died yesterday in California. He was alone over there, never married and I don't know if he had any friends. A social worker called me. I never even got her name straight. She called from Bell Gardens and said Theodore was in the morgue and for me to please find some way of providing for his burial. Although my family lives in El Paso, our parents live across the border in Juarez, Mexico, so we would like to bury Theodore there. The social worker said it would probably cost over $800 to bring the body home. We took up a collection in all the family and raised $450. Can you help us get the body back for less than $800? Can you help us get the body back?

MRS. LEE: You say that you didn't catch the name of the social worker who called you?

MR. RODRIGUEZ: I'm very sorry. I do not know the name of the social worker.

MRS. LEE: That's all right. Let's try to tackle and solve this problem. Here is the situation as I understand it: (1) your brother's body is in a California morgue and we need to bring Theodore back here, (2) a social worker we can't identify at the moment said it would cost over $800 to do this; you have only $450, and neither of us knows how to go about arranging this movement right now, and (3) we need to solve this problem quickly. Is there anything you want to add to this?

MR. RODRIGUEZ: Well, trying to get Theodore's body across the border creates special problems.

MRS. LEE: OK, we will have to check with immigration officials and see how this might be handled.

MR. RODRIGUEZ: I wonder if we should contact some airlines?

MRS. LEE: Good idea. Let's think of as many things to do as possible. We need to locate the social worker, contact the morgue, see what the airlines have to say, and call immigration. Can you think of anything else?

MR. RODRIGUEZ: Oh yes, I forgot, the social worker said it was illegal to transport a body unless you are a funeral home.

MRS. LEE: All right, let's start by calling a funeral home here and see what ideas they can give us.

Mrs. Lee then called one funeral home, which was not very cooperative, but a second funeral home indicated that it had some experience with this kind of problem and could take care of it. Cost would be $550. After talking further with Mr. Rodriguez, Mrs. Lee explained the financial dilemma and the home agreed to do it for $450. The funeral home contacted the California morgue, made all arrangements, and sent a limousine to transfer Theodore's body to Mexico after confirming with immigration. The problem was solved.

We can now study some of the motivational dynamics that underlie Mrs. Lee's problem-solving 9,9 orientation to what might have become an otherwise very serious problem. A 9,9 orientation presumes an inherent *connection* between problem solving and client welfare. Mr. Rodriguez actively participated in solving the problem presented here. Their joint effort helped solve the problem and the client also felt better through having been helped to take a truly responsible action. A 9,9-oriented caseworker desires to get success through involvement. This helped Mr. Rodriguez volunteer ideas and take some responsibility. There was no 9,1-oriented "take over" of the case by the social worker, no 1,9-oriented involvement with the client's sad feelings, no 1,1-oriented feelings of "I don't know what we can do under these circumstances," and no 5,5-oriented discussion about formula or precedents for dealing with this kind of case.

9,9-achievement motivation comes from developing the competence needed to make a contribution through problem solving. If Mrs. Lee had not entered fully into the problem she might have experienced more than momentary failure and have felt some disappointment or discouragement. This caseworker believes that "with caring, commitment, and versatility, we can solve the really tough problems."

Mrs. Lee was not reluctant in a selfish way to face a new and difficult situation. She quickly involved herself and Mr. Rodriguez in identifying the problem clearly and in seeking all possible options. They pursued this problem with vigor and enthusiasm. She took a positive view and did not "refer" the client elsewhere simply because her agency had not handled this type of problem before.

Social Worker Behaviors

A 9,9-oriented caseworker thinks "My job is to make decisions with my client's involvement if he or she is able to participate and for my client if not; but it is important to see, in either case, that sound decisions are made." This style is seen in the following approaches.

> PLANNING. "I get clients to review the whole picture. We formulate a sound model from start to completion to provide a framework for integrating what we are trying to do. I get their reactions and ideas, and we establish goals and flexible steps to help achieve the goals whenever it is possible for them to participate."
>
> ORGANIZING. "Within the framework we have established, we determine our joint and individual responsibilities, procedures, and expectations."
>
> DIRECTING. "I keep informed of client progress and seek to influence this by identifying problems and revising goals *with* them. I lend assistance by helping to remove blocks to progress."
>
> CONTROLLING. "In addition to in-progress critiques about our casework efforts, I conduct a "wrap up" with the client. We evaluate the way things have gone and see what we can learn from our experience and how we can apply this in the future."

The rationale behind these behaviors stem from a 9,9-oriented social worker's belief that when a client is oriented toward achieving a concrete and specific goal that he or she understands and agrees with, his or her behavior becomes more orderly, meaningful, and purposeful.[4] Unlike the views of the client associated with other casework styles, the assumptions underlying a 9,9-oriented approach attest to the basic similarities of all persons. Individual differences are recognized but not

---

[4]Analyses of properties of 9,9-oriented goals are available in Dewey, J. *Democracy and Education.* New York: MacMillan, 1944, pp. 100-110; Sherif, M. and C. Sherif, *An Outline of Social Psychology* (rev. ed.). New York: Harper, 1956, pp. 152-156, 194, 230, 317-330; Sherif, M., O. J. Harvey, B. J. White, W. R. Hood, and C. Sherif, "Intergroup Conflict and Cooperation: The Robbers Cave Experiment." Norman, Okla.: Institute of Group Relations, 1961, pp. 159-197; Krech, D., R. S. Crutchfield, and E. L. Ballachey, *Individual in Society.* New York: McGraw-Hill, 1962, pp. 398-402.

used as excuses to explain troublesome behavior. The client is thought of as a learner who has found ways of trying to satisfy needs through experience with a particular reference group or culture.

The social worker takes an educational posture through a theory/principles intervention with the client when he or she conveys ideas to help the client "see" the situation from a different perspective. With increased understanding, the client is likely to be able to see a wider range of alternative solutions for his or her problems as well as to weigh the probable consequences of each one before selecting the best. In addition, the client is in a better position to apply the principles to other similar problems as they arise in the future. Then a contribution also has been made to the client's problem-solving capability.

The 9,9-oriented social worker has faith in the proposition that if the client has learned disabling behavior patterns in the past it should be possible to help him or her unlearn these patterns and relearn different behaviors that are more productive and satisfying. A confrontation intervention by the 9,9-oriented caseworker can help a client to become more aware of unexamined values or assumptions on which personal behavior rests. This can be accomplished not by criticism or direction, but by challenging a client to see how his or her thinking may be coloring or warping his or her view of a situation. The caseworker behaves in a manner designed to create conditions that help the client become motivated to change.

Focus

We have already noted how various caseworkers tend to focus the caseworker-client relationship. 9,1-oriented caseworkers concentrate mainly on themselves; 1,9-oriented workers focus heavily on the client; 1,1-oriented workers are mostly unfocused, while 5,5-oriented caseworkers are said to fix on an attractive relationship with the client. If you are utilizing a 9,9-oriented casework style, you focus on solving the problem that brings you and your client together. Note how Mrs. Lee focused on making sure that everything was known about the problem surrounding Theodore's death, discussed all possibilities with Mr. Rodriguez, and inquired "Is there anything else?"

This is a crucial point in 9,9 style casework. The principal emphasis is on what is transpiring between the client and yourself in removing barriers and in pursuit of a solution to a real problem. This is exactly what Mrs. Lee did. In daily practice this means dealing with whatever seems to be the most compelling activity, whether someone is depressed, feeling hostile, or very anxious; that is what 9,9-oriented caseworkers focus on — NOW! You get the client to tell you what he or she is doing about it, how it is working out after a period of time, and what you and the client agree ought to be tried next. If there are no deep behavioral dynamics involved, as in Mr. Rodriguez' case, then focus is centered on the problem that needs to be solved.

This means first that you and the client focus on some goals. You may have to confront or challenge more than a little, even though the client may resist, feel a little anxious, and wonder about you. There is nothing that says the client always has to be happy. If the client were happy, he or she probably would not be on your caseload. You may challenge the client to set goals, realistic ones, even though they may be difficult to reach. As a 9,9-oriented caseworker you make sure that goals have the possibility of some success. Few things are more destructive than setting up a client for failure because success options were missing. You help him or her overcome reservations and doubts. Most importantly, you help the client identify actions and select behaviors that are most likely to attain these goals.[5]

When you employ a 9,9-oriented focus, you are looking at the current behavior exhibited by your client. The past is important, but it is not necessarily the "cause" for what the client does now. The relative importance of past history is one of the more controversial points among social work practitioners. Those of you with a Freudian orientation attach considerable significance to the development of a client's personality. A 1,9-

[5]Research pertinent to goal clarity appears in Lewin, K., op. cit., 1951, p. 255; Raven, B. H. and J. Rietsema, "The Effects of Varied Clarity of Group Goal and Group Path Upon the Individual and His Relation to His Group." *Human Relations,* 10 (1957) pp. 29-44; Cohen, A. R. "Situational Structure, Self-Esteem, and Threat-Oriented Reactions to Power." In D. Cartwright (Ed.), op. cit., pp. 35-52; and Gerard, H. B. "Some Effects of Status, Role Clarity, and Group Goal Clarity Upon the Individual's Relations to Group Process." *Journal of Personality,* 25, (1957) pp. 475-488.

oriented caseworker does this routinely in seeking to understand the details and implications of prior events. Thus the 1,9-oriented caseworker in Chapter 4 found it necessary to focus on Mrs. Marshall's past history of relationships with her mother as a way of getting her to understand her depression. A 9,9-oriented worker might have dealt with the pragmatics of homemaker services and other "here and now" aspects of helping Mrs. Marshall's disabled mother as a way of dealing with that part of Mrs. Marshall's depression. While there are viewpoints which differ from this approach, 9,9-oriented workers tend to stress the dynamics of "now" events. When you do this you are asking your client to think about whether or not his or her current activities are in line with the goals you agreed upon.

One expert encouraging the latter point of view is Glasser,[6] whose ideas are a must in your reading.

Power Uses

The most direct thing that can be said about this matter is that 9,9-oriented social workers share their power by concentrating it on solving the problem with clients. This may seem like a sound idea, but what does it mean? It means you recognize that ultimately it is up to the client to change. Therefore, he or she already has the power but in your relationship you redirect it to the problem and add your assistance to help the client solve it. You have not given power to the client, for he or she already owns it. What you have done is to harness and concentrate this power toward the goal of change through problem solving.

You will also share your effort with other sources in the client's environment, including friends, relatives, employers, or anyone you recognize as a potential helper in your client's life. If the client is to be in any degree responsible for his or her own behavior, he or she must help create that behavior because people cannot be held responsible for what they did not help create. This is also one of Glasser's main points. If you help the

[6]Glasser, William, *Reality Therapy*. New York: Harper and Row, 1964.

client identify what he or she thinks is important, and if you also agree with it, it is perfectly all right to hold the client to that behavior. This is a tangible way of insisting on problem solving, not to what you as a 9,1-oriented worker might decree, but to a goal which the client has indicated that he or she values in some way. Such strategy is an example of concentrating power on problem solving.

A 9,9-oriented social worker dealing with Mr. Jones, the elderly black man encountered in Chapters 4 and 5, might have said, "OK, Mr. Jones, you do not want to live in a housing project, so you must decide where you really do want to live. Let's explore possibilities other than the project, which will help you make that decision."

As a caseworker, when you operate according to a 9,9 orientation, your source of power is drawn from your knowledge or expertise and from the confidence the client places in you. The client responds to your power not because he or she fears you in a 9,1 way, not because he or she wants rewarding love and affection in a 1,9 way, not because of your title as in a 1,1 orientation, and not because he or she finds you attractive in a 5,5 sense, but mainly because you come through as knowing what you are doing and caring about the client.

If you truly help the client practice what you preach, in his or her own way the client will become involved. To that extent he or she also is likely to become committed to this kind of problem-solving approach to change.

In considering how a caseworker uses power, the possibility of caseworker-client conflict, either subtle or overt, must be considered. Conflict might delay the attainment of casework goals but it might also produce new ideas and enhance the casework relationship. The key is in how conflict is managed by the caseworker. There are several 9,9 approaches to this matter.

One approach is for the worker to communicate openly and to encourage the same from a client. The remark "In the final analysis, words have little meanings, it is only people who have meanings" is a 9,9 description. Words are tools for achieving interaction. There is no problem of communication, per se. There are problems of people who work together in trying to communicate with each other. Rationalization, projection, compensation, and other widely known defense mechanisms enter into the casework process. The power that a caseworker has and the way he or she uses it is a key to open communication. If you say to your client "I am interested in your ideas," the client is more likely to be able to express reservations and doubts and to contribute ideas.

If the social worker seeks a great deal of information but gives little, the casework relationship is likely to be unstable. It is likely to drift in the direction of neither giving nor getting much. Openness stimulates trust; closedness fosters lack of trust. If the caseworker genuinely wants to know what is going on, he or she needs to relate forthrightly what he or she understands the situation to be. This is *leveling*. Once conditions promoting full disclosure have been achieved, there are few reasons for misunderstandings, for withholding negative information, or for the many other communication pitfalls that prevent effective two-way interactions.

A 9,9-oriented caseworker also explains the rationale behind requests of the client. When the client is stimulated to think, analyze, evaluate, and see cause-and-effect relationships, he or she can respond constructively to caseworker requests.

When differences between social worker and client do appear, a 9,9-oriented social worker looks for facts, data, and logic to resolve them. As a result, answers to complex questions are likely to be approached from an attitude of fact finding. Since finding a best solution is his or her objective, there is less need to deny, distort, or defend his or her own position.

Critique is crucial in managing and resolving worker-client conflict, or agency-related conflict.[7] It involves people in analyzing an activity and sharing their reactions to it in an open and constructive way. Critique can reveal weaknesses, doubts, and reservations that might otherwise remain hidden. These can be discussed and dealt with in a problem-solving way because each person's insights are compared and evaluated. With this approach it is often necessary to use confrontation as a

[7]A comprehensive study of critique methodologies is in Blake, R. R. and J. S. Mouton, *Making Experience Work: The Grid Approach to Critique*. New York: McGraw-Hill, 1978.

means of focusing on antagonisms that are created by strong win-lose kinds of disagreement, facing up to them, and bringing them out into the open where they can be resolved directly by those who are a party to them.[8]

Dependence

One of the most essential elements in 9,9-oriented casework is that the client must test reality for any behavioral change being considered before it is adopted. In other words, he or she has to try the thing out to see if "it works" in order to determine if it is helpful. If you suggest that your client attempt a particular behavior for thirty days to see if it brings different reactions from others, the client must be free to experiment in his or her own way. You are there supporting and encouraging but the client must take the final responsibility to try. This means the client is not dependent on you. His or her activities are dependent on the process or outcome of what he or she is doing in life, not on anything else.

In 9,9-oriented practice there is only minimal dependence on the social worker. The client expects your encouragement and expects you to have other ideas when his or her attempts at different behaviors are not effective and the problem continues. Mr. Rodriguez conceivably might have become dependent on Mrs. Lee's assistance, but this never occurred. She called on him for suggestions, probed with him to clarify as much as possible, kept the casework tempo going, and kept Mr. Rodriguez' spirit "up" through a very distressing time. There was no time for him to become dependent. After the logistics of burial were attended to, it might be appropriate to consider his emotional situation, if he so desires, as this is most often the point at which emotions related to loss of loved ones appear.

Interviewing and Recording

When a 9,9-oriented caseworker interviews, he or she is likely to be objective in the sense of examining both facts and emo-

---

[8]An extensive study of confrontation for value clarification is contained in Blake, R. R. and J. S. Mouton, *Consultation*. Reading, Mass.: Addison-Wesley, 1976, pp. 224-226.

tions. This means that you retain sensitivity to feelings while getting important facts as well. A 9,9 orientation does not emphasize factual information to the exclusion of emotions as do the 9,1 and 1,1 orientations, but neither does it elevate feelings to a position more important than facts. It may be said that "feelings are facts." If your client has a certain emotion at any given moment, that becomes a "fact," and the 9,9-oriented caseworker relates to it in that manner. If your client quit his job and is now feeling sorry and guilty about it, you might ask these kinds of questions:

"Tell me, what are some of the reasons you didn't like the job?"

"What were your wife's reactions when you quit?"

"What are you doing now for a job?"

Your interviewing style avoids yes-no responses and is characterized by queries that help the client think through his or her situation to explore alternatives that might contribute to a solution. You seek to get both sides of every story and are not overly quick to identify with your client's feelings.

You see the importance of "why" questions but may place more emphasis on "what" questions. If your client is running with the wrong crowd you might ask, for example, "What is it about this group that attracts you so much?" or "I know it's hard to stay away from those groups," rather than "Why in the world are you hanging around with those guys?" Very often too much attention is paid to "why" questions, which only give you reasons or rationalizations for what the client is doing. Many of them have spent large parts of their lives rationalizing away their activities. If you encourage clients to discuss current happenings you are more likely to succeed in having them face up to their behaviors.

9,9-oriented social workers are concerned with *now* behaviors when they interview and record. Historical information is put into perspective and not necessarily used to explain current activities. The possible consequences of what your client presently is engaged in doing may provide many opportunities for you to convey information to him or her about positive and negative aspects of new activities.

Providing information to the client is very important to a

9,9-oriented caseworker. He or she recognizes that certain problems clients present are solved or neutralized when proper information is available. Getting the client to see events from a different point of view or to consider the weight of data can influence a shift in the frame of reference he or she has been employing.

Records are kept brief to reflect only salient points. Information tends to be conceptualized, as 9,9-oriented caseworkers make tentative judgments about what they are seeing and reducing to paper. 9,9-oriented caseworkers, therefore, tend to use information only when it seems to have shaped the client's behavior in some way. If you are trying to convey understanding of a client who has been, say, shoplifting, you might record the date and time of each instance. A 9,9-oriented kind of record might say "The client was arrested twice in the past nine months for shoplifting, a behavior which had not occurred prior to her husband's death one year ago, and there may be some connection here that needs further study."

9,9-oriented social work practice can be examined further in the following interaction between seventeen-year-old Mary Williamson and her social worker, Ms. Glasby, which covers a six-week period. Mary has had a history of problematic behavior since age thirteen. She engaged in such delinquent behavior as running away from home, shoplifting, sexual promiscuity, and the use of alcohol. Mary was eventually sent to the state industrial school for girls by the juvenile court. She spent several months at that school and has now been released on parole or aftercare.

The social worker is a graduate student in practicum. The case emphasizes casework dynamics that occur between social worker and client rather than historical/developmental information. Mary brings chronic hostility to the casework situation, together with a low self-image and considerable difficulty in trusting others.

TELEPHONE

10-4. Mary called re: her 2:00 PM appointment. She said that five hundred things had come up, and she was unable to get to the office at 2:00 (this was 3:30). I asked if there was any reason why she could not come at 4:00. She said she could come at 4:00.

OFFICE

10-4. Mary came in at 4:55. She said she got tangled up in transportation and forgot to get off the bus. The driver had promised to let her off at Forshey Street, but he forgot to do so.

I said that such a mix-up could make her feel upset and angry. She said "yeah." Mary was dressed very sophisticatedly and chain smoked throughout our contact.

I explained my role. Mary said she knew I was a student social worker. I said that she might feel like a student was objectional as a caseworker in her situation. I tried to present my competence. I got the feeling that she was very interested in me, but she wanted to appear as if she didn't care.

We started to arrange an appointment time. She said, "Ms. Glasby, I might as well be truthful. It's the best way to be." Me: "What is it?" Mary: "I'm working at a drive-in restaurant." Then she went on to say she works from 4:00 to 12:00. Her mother walks home with her. The employer has promised her a 7:00-4:00 shift. She likes the job. This complicated our schedule. It finally worked out I could see her from 12:00 to 1:00 on Thursdays.

We talked about her former experience with casework. She seemed to have a positive attitude. I knew that she had some good and bad experiences at the state school. She made no comment.

I said that she told the social worker at school that she was not sure about how successful her parole would be. Mary denied any problems at home or elsewhere.

This interview lasted 30 minutes. I sensed resistance on Mary's part. I felt that my own attitude was very much evident. I felt provoked because of the time Mary got to the office. I also had an appointment at 6:00 and felt rushed to make that appointment.

When Mary got up to leave, she didn't know what bus to catch. Since I was going to her neighborhood, I suggested she ride with me. Also, another worker rode part of the way. Mary said very little as we drove home. She could not define her own feelings very well, but she did add that she was "as good as anyone." She did bring out that she felt others didn't feel she was "as good as they are," because she lives in a housing project.

I sensed that this girl has a very poor self-image. She feels inferior and compensates with a stab at sophistication and an "I-don't-care" attitude.

Home Visit

10-11. I visited the home of Mary by pre-arranged appointment. I knocked and a man's voice said, "Let her in. She probably wants to see Mary." A woman answered in a loud hostile voice, "I'm not having any damn snooper around here!" I knocked four more times. The apartment got very quiet, and no one answered the knock.

When I got back to the office, Mary had called. She left a message that said, "She had to leave home to buy a pair of shoes for work tomorrow." The call came one hour after I had been at her home.

On this same date I wrote Mary and her mother asking them to come to the office on October 18 at 4:00.

Telephone

10-16. Mrs. Williamson called, but I was out. She said Mary was working on Thursday, could not get off the job, and could not be contacted at work.

Office Visit

10-18. Mrs. Williamson came in at 1:30. Her appointment was at 4:00. She initiated the interview by saying she came to tell me Mary couldn't come because she had to work. She said they were both sick with colds on Monday and Tuesday. She herself was still sick. She pointed to her mouth which was covered with fever blisters, saying she always got them when she had a fever. Since Mary had been sick, she had to work on a day when she was usually off.

I said I was sorry I missed seeing them when I made a home visit. She said, "We waited until 3:30, then Mary went to get shoes." She couldn't understand why she had not heard my knock. I told her what I heard through the door. She neither denied nor affirmed it, but stated that I must have been at the back door and not the front. I mentioned Mary's 12:50 call saying she had not been home during my visit. Mrs. Williamson evaded, lied, and defended. I didn't push and remained pleasant. I asked why Mary could not keep her appointment today, and was told she was working from 7:00 to 3:00. I still didn't understand why she couldn't come.

Mrs. Williamson said that she didn't want Mary to lose her job. How often did I want to see her? She frowned when I said once a week. She said she thought Mary had paid her debt when she was at the state school. I said Mary wasn't paying a debt; I merely wanted to see her. She was on parole and was obligated to see me.

Mrs. Williamson said she was afraid Mary would lose her job. She liked it and seemed happy. I assured her I was pleased with the job and would not cause Mary to lose her job. I just wanted to see her.

Mrs. Williamson said that Mary was doing well. I said that I was glad to hear this. However, I wanted to talk with her.

Mrs. Williamson was frowning and, I felt, trying to see if I would change my mind. She was not hostile — rather, passive and then aggressive.

I said that I felt Mary didn't want to come, and I could certainly understand that. Perhaps she was afraid.

(Mrs. Williamson was quite serious in tone. She was trying to let me understand.) She leaned over my desk and said, "I don't want you to push Mary too hard. She can't be pushed. She thinks everyone is down on her. She feels people are out to get her. She is afraid to come. She doesn't like people telling her what to do. She has said this time and time again."

I said that the only thing I knew about Mary is she doesn't like the housing project. Yes, this was true. She has begged her mother to move. She hates the project. Mary's mother didn't know why — perhaps the people.

I said Mary got along well with the caseworker at the state school. Yes, she loved the worker. She has written to her and would like to visit her. She helped Mary a lot. I said that I wanted to help Mary, too, but I didn't know how unless she came into the office. She didn't trust people much, I had observed. Mrs. Williamson said this was true. She said this was bad for Mary — "Mary believes everyone is out to get her."

I said these are the sort of things I wanted to talk about, too. I told her Mary had a responsibility to come. I said that Mrs. Williamson and I knew how important it was for Mary to see me. But it was up to us to convince her that it was important. I pointed out that Mrs. Williamson could use her own understanding to help Mary get into the office. Here I was trying to bring Mrs. Williamson into the act, so to speak, and give her a feeling that we were working together to help Mary.

During this interview, I said several times that Mary was required to come in to see me. I reiterated that I didn't want to hurt Mary and that Mary was hurting herself by not coming in. I pointed out the legal aspects of the situation.

I felt when Mrs. Williamson left that she had warmed up to me. She was still tense and fearful about the situation, but she did respond well to me.

At the end of the interview, I said Mary would be expected Thursday. It would be her responsibility to contact me on Thursday to say what time she was coming. Mrs. Williamson blocked this again by saying that she would call if Mary could not come. I said I wanted Mary to both call and come. I said I would keep in touch with Mrs. Williamson. I suggested Mrs. Williamson contact me any time about questions or concerns about Mary. But I could not let her be a substitute for Mary and assume Mary's responsibility.

During this interview, I tried to relay my acceptance and understanding of the resistance. Yet I remained firm about what I was asking of the client.

Office Visit

10-25. Mary had telephoned on 10-22. She sounded like she didn't care but she more or less agreed to see me on 10-25.

She was early for her appointment. The first thing she did was to give me some gum. We began to discuss her job, which she had quit because it was too far from home. She had looked for another job, but so far no luck.

I commented on my talk with her mother. I said that I got the impression Mrs. Williamson was afraid I would hurt Mary. Mary explained that her mother is obsessed with this idea. But Mary told her she could take care of herself. I said: "What does she think will hurt you?" Mary: "You all will send me back to the state school."

Question by question, I gained a glimpse of Mary's life. Her existence was a struggle. Mary: "I have a struggle with authority, but I keep my mouth shut now." Me: "Who said this?" Mary: "I know this. I read a lot."

Between each question, I had time to elaborate. She just chewed gum and looked at her feet.

Mary: "What have you got in that record on me?" I told her and she looked at the type of forms, but she didn't read them. Mary: "How come you got all this time to work with me? How come someone like you works with me?" I told her that the case was referred to me because she needed help, wanted help, and could make use of help, as she had used the worker at the school.

I asked Mary what she liked to read, since about the only thing I really knew at this point was her interest in reading. She told me she liked poetry. She sort of liked educational things. At this point she told about her steady boy friend. He sounded like a bum. They argue a lot.

Mary said next "The first time I saw you I thought I couldn't stand you." Why did she think that? She didn't know. We discussed what had happened. I told her I was pretty upset because she waited so long to come that day. She said "I was mad because I had to come. I guess I was mad and took it out on you." Me: "I think you're right. People often do this." Mary: "Do you think it will happen again?" Me: "Let's wait and see."

Then Mary told me of her great love for her caseworker at the state school. She said "I hated her at first, but you won't believe that I cried when I had to leave." I made no comment.

Mary: "Did you know I raised hell before I left the school?" Me: "Yes." Mary: "Do you know why I did this?" Me: "No. Maybe we can talk about this, next time, if you want to." Mary: "I'll bet you know why I didn't want to become involved with another social worker."

The interview lasted over an hour. I commented that we seemed to have a lot of things to talk about. Mary said she would be willing to see how things went. I said I wanted her to come in again.

I was impressed by Mary's ability to discuss things intelligently. The school had given her a low-average intelligence score.

I like her much better this time, and felt she was more willing to engage in conversation. It was a strenuous interview.

Office Visit

11-8. Mary came in on time.

I picked up where we left off last time — about life in the training school. Mary described in great detail her experience. She pointed out that she was now better able to understand what went on. She repeated several times that she realizes they were trying to help her, although she didn't think so at the time. She progressed to her relationship with her caseworker. She again said she had a hard time relating to the worker until she got to know her. I related that to the relationship between Mary and me. We talked about "trust." Mary said that she did not yet trust me. I said I felt this, but I didn't expect her to come in and trust me right away. She asked if I wrote down what she said. I showed her my yellow tablet and said that I put down the important things so that I could think about our talks and remember things we might want to talk about in the future. She asked if I put it in the record. I said no, only the part which would show that she was present, participating, and what direction our work together was taking. I asked if she kept notes. She seemed surprised. I said that she might find this was fun to write up our talks together. She could put down what she said and what I said. She said she might try it.

Mary again brought out her fear of being returned. I made a connection between her reservations about talking and her fear of return to the state school. She said, "Yes, this does enter in."

I got out the sheet with the conditions of parole. I read over them and asked about the regulation which was hardest to keep. Mary said: "Stay away from bad company." Mary went into a pretty long discussion of "bad company." We talked about what kind of company is "bad for her." I realized that Mary had a problem in this area. She operated within a circle of young people who were on probation and parole. In her discussions, she brought out a most interesting and thorough knowledge of B-drinking (a minor soliciting drinks from adults in bars). She asked, at one point, what I would do if I saw her in a bar. I said I would encourage her to leave because there was always the possibility of a police raid. I said I thought a bar was the worst place she could be at this point in her life.

I listened to Mary's discussion of her friends, without judgment. I commented on the problem and suggested this was something we would want to talk about from time to time.

Time was up. Mary said she had read an article on out-of-wedlock pregnancy and what it means. We discussed briefly her feelings about why a girl would get pregnant out-of-wedlock. Finally we reached a point of saying that this was another way to get back at the authority of our parents and society.

Mary said she loved to read about psychology — about what can cause people to go wrong. She said she couldn't get books about this and asked if I would bring her one. I said I'd like to, but I wondered about the wisdom of this. I said people who read medical books often thought they had the various medical illnesses. People who read psychology might feel they have certain emotional problems. This was not good. Mary gave an expression of disgust and said, "Miss Glasby, I am not that big a baby." She said she'd be careful. I said I would lend her a book if I could find one that would hold her interest and was not too complex.

Mary left in good spirits. I felt that she had stated her position about engaging herself to me and revealing herself. I responded with recognition and acceptance of her thinking, keeping a focus on what we hoped would develop into positive results.

Office Visit

11-15. Mary was on time for her interview. I noted she was dressed more appropriately for her age. She began by saying that she tried to remember what we had planned to discuss this time, but she could not.

I had planned to have a more controlled type of interview; that is, I thought we had been discussing on too general a level. I wanted to go into more detail about some aspects of Mary's day-to-day living. I wanted to know how she really operated. I had not really challenged her on her descriptions and comments. I wanted to move in a little closer to some of her defenses.

I began to talk about what she plans to do about a job,

getting money — problems in this area. She said she really wasn't interested in work. What about money? Yes, she refused to ask her parents for money. She really felt that employers were out to get her. They wanted her to grovel for a job. She lied to them about being on probation. She has pondered what to do about Christmas money. I gave her the address for the State Employment Service and suggested she contact them. "Well, I really can't do anything," said Mary. I suggested a trade school. She said she couldn't stand school confinement. "I have this conflict with authority."

I really pushed her to tell me about the "conflict with authority." She could not explain, except to say she was "defiant." Mary said, "You're supposed to know what I mean." Me: "I'm interested in what you think you mean."

We naturally directed our attention to her handling of herself. I learned she can only respond by hostility. She cried sometimes and would withdraw from conflict. We explored her behavior when she got mad. She was unable to distinguish her always hostile responses.

Mary: "What is your opinion of me?" Me: "I only know what you tell me." Mary: "I'm interested in what you have concluded." Me: "What do you want me to think?" Mary: "That I'm normal as anybody; everyone has problems." Me: "I think you have some problems." Mary: "What?" Me: "We've discussed that you don't trust people." Mary: "I have some people who are my friends. What do you think I am like?" Me: "I think you are a girl who is active with people. You have friends — you laugh, dance, goof off. But you never get too close. These people don't touch you in any way. Your closest associate could drop dead and I doubt you would cry." Mary: "I don't care enough to wear black for anyone." (She let this drop.) Me: "You shut yourself out from people."

Mary was very quiet; for the first time she seemed vulnerable.

Me: "What does this mean?" Mary shrugged. Me: "Is this good? What does the future hold for you?" She smiled.

Me: "This is a problem we can talk about after you think on it awhile."

In this situation Mary was uncooperative and rebellious from the outset, despite being on official parole. The social worker was able to accept Mary's feelings and understand her hostile behavior until the girl was able to deal with her frustration. Such an acceptant strategy allowed Mary to express negative emotions without rejection. Soon Mary was able to ask "How come someone like you works with me?" This provided the first opening for Ms. Glasby to elicit a response from Mary.

From then on the interaction began to assume 9,9 qualities such as —

"I have a problem with authority."

"The first time I saw you I thought I couldn't stand you."

"What would you do if you saw me in a bar?"

"What is your opinion of me?"

"You laugh, dance, goof off but you never get too close."

"Your closest associate could drop dead and I doubt you would cry."

These are all examples of open direct expression of ideas and feelings of great importance. They symbolize the most crucial dynamics to be dealt with and solved. These dynamics would probably not have emerged without the 9,9-oriented credibility which Ms. Glasby was able to acquire once Mary freed herself of disabling emotions.

The social worker's early focus seemed to be on Mary's feelings and on gaining friendly acceptance from both Mary and her mother. Gradually this focus shifted to the content of what was being discussed and Mary responded to this by doing likewise.

Although the social worker had official power she chose not to invoke it too soon. When she took out the conditions of parole and read them to Mary they had already begun a solid relationship. These rules were less threatening to Mary because of the relationship, and interviewing was on the basis of problems to be solved rather than on who was on top of them.

After six weeks it seemed evident that Mary had undergone significant changes in dress and in attitude toward herself, toward her social worker, and toward the set of conditions that brought her to the agency.

Ms. Glasby and Mary continued to have conferences. The situation as it now exists is that, while Mary is not the town's most illustrious citizen, she has learned to cope effectively with the problems of living. She has had no further difficulty in terms of legal considerations. Married and later divorced, she has held a responsible job and takes care of her child.

Agency Personality

Social workers are likely to enjoy working in a 9,9-oriented agency. One of the things first noticed about such agencies is that there is a high level of participation by staff in the various agency activities. The bosses do not always think it necessary to make decisions themselves but do see to it that decisions are made. Staff input is important to 9,9-oriented administrators, who believe that participation increases staff support for agency goals. The program then is characterized by realistic goals, which staff members have helped establish, and there is a sense of teamwork in goal pursuit.

Other signs of a 9,9 orientation include consistent and continuing evaluation of what goes on in the program. Again, staff social workers contribute to an understanding of how services might be improved by identifying weaknesses that have cropped up. Because caseworkers often lead these meetings, the regularly held staff meetings are not devoted exclusively to administrative announcements.

The kind of supervision offered is another sign of a 9,9 orientation. 9,1 supervision, for example, is "centralized" in the supervisor, and workers end up saying "The supervisor is responsible, not me." This abdication of responsibility is unlike the 9,9 outcome, where supervisors use a participative style that helps establish directions for the caseworker who then operates autonomously and with consequent responsibility for what happens.

If you are in a 9,9-oriented agency you may also note that full disclosure of agency matters seems to be a norm. Little or no gamesmanship occurs and social workers do not have to play it "close to the vest." When conflict arises, agency climate allows you to "put your cards on the table." This confrontation approach is generally used to solve disagreements.

9,9-oriented agencies take ideas from the socio/behavioral sciences and attempt to put these ideas to use. This is all another way of saying that 9,9-oriented agencies are change-oriented.

You know that you are in a 9,9-oriented agency if you are encouraged to use innovative approaches in your casework practice. 9,9 environments foster experimentation, some open-endedness in service delivery, and a willingness to take some measured risks.

Client Reactions

The 9,9 way of integrating clients into problem solving is consistent with sound behavioral science principles as applied to casework. For this reason clients might be expected to react to this casework approach with enthusiasm, and some do. However, this is not always the case, particularly in the beginning.

Many caseworkers have never had a real experience with a 9,9 way of doing casework and, therefore, are not in the position to evaluate it in comparison to their experiences with other ways. They have learned to regard 9,9 as unrealistic from earlier experiences with difficult cases, and they simply are unwilling to approach their clients in this way. Thus clients cannot react to something they have not experienced.

One reaction among clients is a readiness to become involved in the casework process and to strive to cooperate with the caseworker. Involvement and commitment are strong indicators that the client is motivated to change. This produces a "can do" spirit in both worker and client.

Another reaction acknowledges that 9,9 collaboration is a good possibility, but that it expects too much of a client, who may want, at least initially, to "give his problem away." The requirements of involvement, participation, and commitment are beyond what the client may wish to do, related to his depression or frustration. This is understandable because the client might prefer to be "helped."

Another reaction is "It's impractical. It takes too much time. It won't work." Some clients have become so conditioned by their caseworker experiences that they dismiss the 9,9 idea as impractical. If this feeling is conveyed to the caseworker, the latter may have to "settle for less" and react to the client on the basis of lowered expectations on the part of each.

Childhood Origins

The key to understanding the kind of child rearing that leads to a 9,9 orientation as an adult is that parents have and implement an explicit and systematic model for the kind of person toward which they intend to guide their child's development. The model contains two components. One is the capacity for autonomy, which means promoting the child's capacity for spontaneity and freedom to act according to his or her own choices. This means guiding the child in self-direction. The other is the capacity for cooperation and mutual respect that can permit sound interactions with other people.[9]

Autonomy

In creating an autonomous environment parents are more concerned with setting the conditions of growth than channeling its direction. They emphasize performance standards and respond to the child's emotions in an accepting and understanding way, but they resist telling the child what his or her emotions should or should not be. The child learns to choose from among alternatives rather than relying on others for counsel and advice. He or she learns to create alternatives by imagining unanticipated possibilities as the capacity to do

---

[9]9,9-oriented child rearing is described as follows. For example, when a child misbehaves, parents are likely to ask why he did so and to help the child see the consequences that happen to other people who behave similarly. Punishment is meted out only when it has been discussed and the reasons for it are well understood. Parents teach the child that he can and should control his own behavior on the basis of an internalized set of standards and norms rather than being controlled based upon parental requirements, peer pressures, or simply getting by; see Douvan, E. and J. Adelson, *The Adolescent Experience.* New York: Wiley, 1966.

Limit-setting by parents is discussed in Dreikurs, R. and L. Grey, *Logical Consequences: A New Approach to Discipline.* New York: Meridith Press, 1968, pp. 62-82.

The positive effects of parent-child cooperation is discussed in Adler, A. *Social Interest: A Challenge to Mankind.* New York: Capricorn Books, 1964, p. 29. See also Dreikurs, R., R. Corsini, and S. Gould, *How to Stop Fighting with Your Kids.* Chicago: Ace Printing, 1974, pp. 49-56.

things continues to progress.

Spontaneity is respected and encouraged within the limits of safety. Children are provided an environment free of dangerous objects, which prevents them from being hurt and which obviates the need for constant warnings. Such parents recognize that punishment which is rational in the sense of being a predictable consequence of infringements serves the purpose of reinforcing limits that parents believe are important enough not to be violated.

9,9-oriented parents know that self-esteem is enhanced in children when they learn to succeed.[10] Thus, they give their children acceptance and support in their efforts to be competent and to contribute.

Cooperation and Mutual Respect

Parents promote cooperation by engaging in give-and-take activities in which both parents and child influence outcomes. Parents and child emphasize cooperation as a source of pleasure. Parents enter the child's world of play with joy and laughter. In this way, other people become a source of interest, challenge, and pleasure.

9,9-oriented parents learn to give love unconditionally and not to meter it out according to the degree of acceptability of the child's behavior. A child learns that human feelings involve caring, which means that others make a difference. The child's feelings about his or her parents are extended to others, including brothers and sisters, neighbors, school mates, and friends. As growth proceeds, there is more understanding of what effective behavior really is. Sharing in work and play, with respect to brothers, sisters, and others, helps children find solutions to problems rather than having requirements im-

---

[10]Evidence that children who are held in esteem by their associates in school come from homes where they enjoy secure and rewarding relationships with parents and brothers and sisters confirms the importance of solid emotional attachments in the home as a precondition for the emergence of a 9,9 orientation. See Campbell, J. D. and M. R. Yarrow, "Perceptual and Behavioral Correlates of Social Effectiveness." *Sociometry,* 24 (1961) pp. 1-20; Maslow, A. H. "Creativity in Self-Actualizing People." In H. H. Anderson (Ed.), *Creativity and Its Cultivation.* New York: Harper, 1959, pp. 85-86, 88; and Sullivan, H. S. *The Interpersonal Theory of Psychiatry.* New York: Norton, 1953.

posed by parents.

This type of child rearing does not eliminate conflict or feelings of anger, fear, and anxiety, but it does reduce conflict between parents and child. Righteous indignation may surface but blind anger and hate are minimized.

Underlying the development of both the capacity for autonomy and for cooperation are four fundamental aspects of teaching and learning. One is that parents regard *learning* as valuable in its own right. Another is that parents use *critique* to help a child see connections between experiences and their consequences. Third, parents use *modeling* to demonstrate behavior, and finally, the child is encouraged to act *independently* or *cooperatively,* depending on the circumstances.

9,9 Goal-Tending

Goal planning and implementation takes on a special significance in 9,9-oriented casework. We would like to elaborate on this under the idea of "9,9 Goal-Tending." This subject is treated differently under the 9,9 way of doing casework than it is with other Grid positions.

Several points must be considered if the caseworker is to use goal-tending with clients in a manner that unites problem-solving concern with concern for the client as an individual.

The first is that the client must feel psychological ownership for the goal, even though the caseworker may propose it. This means that the client is motivated to be autonomous and to reach a goal when it belongs to him or her. Then the client is involved in being successful by applying energies to reach that goal. Again, note how Mrs. Lee got Mr. Rodriguez to pursue the goal of getting Theodore's body back quickly even when the situation appeared so complex to the client. Mr. Rodriguez continued to feel the goal to be his own, even though Mrs. Lee became very central in finding a solution.

Second, a good goal, one that motivates change, has clarity for the client. Though a goal may be perfectly clear to the caseworker, it may not be to the client, who is likely to resist it because it makes no sense to him or her. When a goal is clear, the client may be able to mobilize scarce energy resources toward accomplishing it.

Another property of a goal is related to the pathway of activity necessary to reach it. What is necessary is a complete and clear understanding on a step-by-step basis of the factors that limit the goal achievement. Then it becomes possible to deal with the limitations in a realistic way and on a one, two, three basis. In dealing with these barriers to goal attainment, caseworkers often are able to get in and help with the real problems facing the client. Ideally the route to a goal, like overcoming depression, inadequate parenting, or poor sexual adjustment, should be thoroughly outlined, but specific steps on that route should be formulated by and with the person responsible for taking them. If some problems are seen as genuinely beyond the client's control, this is understood and additional help or support can be provided. There is no need for the caseworker to lower goals of service excellence. What is necessary is that any gap between achievement and excellence needs to be clearly understood, anticipated, and provided for by both the worker and the client.

Goal setting is a way of changing, by foresight, what needs to be done to reach some objective. Thus in Chapter 3 we encountered Mrs. Blair who needed to come to terms with caring for her children. In Chapter 4, Mrs. Marshall had to overcome her depression about her invalid mother. In Chapter 5, Mrs. Muñoz required straight help to secure food stamps. In Chapter 6, we saw the Fergusons with a goal of improving their marital sex life, and Chapter 7 we met Mr. Rodriguez with a goal of getting his deceased brother's body back home and buried in a dignified manner. Without the clarification of foresight through goal-tending, all of these client goals might not have been accomplished. When their goals are clear, with explicit steps necessary for reaching them formulated, actual progress is possible.

The time span for reaching goals is another significant property of 9,9-oriented casework. A client may allow too much time, or too little, between setting a goal and accomplishing it. Goals that are too distant have the disadvantage of being unrelated to current activities. An immediate goal may not be motivating because time is so short as to render the goal unachievable, or if it can be attained almost immediately, it may be seen as unchallenging and not worthy of accomplishment.

In terms of goal setting, the social worker needs to decide "how good is good." How "good" a mother should Mrs. Blair become? How "good" should Mrs. Marshall be in overcoming her depression? These are practical, goal-oriented issues. The best standard is excellence. Excellence means "If that goal were to be reached, the problem would be solved" or "That is a true solution" or "This is the most we can accomplish under the actual conditions faced by Mrs. Blair or Mrs. Marshall." Another way of characterizing excellence is to say what it is not. "That is a little better than I had expected from Mrs. Blair." Excellence, in other words, is the best that rigorous thinking and analysis can visualize. Often goals based on excellence are really no more difficult to achieve and are more rewarding to reach.

Feedback to the client on his or her performance is another factor in 9,9-oriented casework. If the client has valid feedback, he or she is able to evaluate whether the goal is being achieved. It becomes more motivating to strive when feedback is available to measure the degree of progress.

Another characteristic of 9,9 goal-tending has been identified as the completion effect. Once a client has accepted the idea of achieving a goal, internal tensions arise toward successful completion. When barriers arise to block this client, he or she does not say "I got blocked," but increases his or her efforts to remove the barrier. These tensions constitute part of the motivating force that explains why committed people do not quit simply because difficulties are encountered.

In sum, it can be said that where there is a high level of client participation and involvement in goal-setting activities, there is an equally high level of commitment to the behaviors deemed necessary for goal attainment.[11] This is what 9,9-oriented caseworkers think and act upon.

---

[11]Coch, L. and J. R. P. French, Jr. "Overcoming Resistance to Change," *Human Relations,* 1 (1948) pp. 512-532.

Implications of 9,9-Oriented Casework

Every social work practitioner tends to have a preferred Grid style and to give this style priority when entering into a helping relationship with clients. This is true of the "dominant" style as well as the "backup" style.

If you adopt a 9,1-oriented approach, be prepared to have to coerce the client and to encounter rebelliousness. If you rely on 1,9-oriented strategies, be ready to accept slow progress by the client, or to see him or her leave prematurely. If you rest on 1,1-oriented casework, be ready to take abuse, see the client leave rather than accept snail-pace progress, or "pray" for spontaneous remission. If a 5,5 casework orientation is your choice, be ready to work within the client frame of reference and be satisfied with small indications of changes that demonstrate the client is moving in what you believe to be the "right" direction. If 9,9 is your casework style, you will have to be knowledgeable, competent, resourceful, and persistent. When the client tries something you suggest and it works, the client is probably going to accept it because he or she experienced the success. The client internalizes the goals, taking them into him- or herself and feeling the satisfaction of having reached them. All of the five Grid-oriented casework strategies promote some kind of change, but positive change is most apt to occur and to endure when it is accepted into the client's frame of reference.

9,9-oriented casework interventions are rooted in ideas which emerge from the behavioral sciences. The two cycle-breaking interventions designed to bring about change are confrontation (which serves to refocus the definition of a problem or reevaluate alternatives) and a theory/principles intervention (where the objective is to introduce problem-solving capability to the client and to open up a range of new possibilities for problem solution, as well as to increase his or her ability to deal with similar problems in the future). Both of these interventions offer good prospects that sound and enduring change can be brought about in the client's behavior. These points are discussed further in Chapter 8 but two examples are pertinent now. One is from social psychology as exemplified by Blake and Mouton. These deal with how you interact with the client.

Another is from psychiatry as illustrated by Glasser and centers on a strategy for getting the client to make progress.

Glasser's work on Reality Therapy seems to represent one way in which to implement the 9,9-oriented casework style. While there are various other routes to the same goal, Glasser's methods can be stressed. He suggests several steps to follow with your client that provide a useful framework when your concerns for problem solving and for the client as an individual are coupled and are of equal importance.

GET INVOLVED. You cannot hope to expect change if you do not establish some rapport with the client. This need not be as emotional as 1,9 or as attractive as 5,5, but something must be there. You ask questions, answer questions, become enthusiastic, show friendliness, and compassion. You must give involvement.

CONCENTRATE ON "NOW." Although past events may be significant, your client's problem is right now. He or she is hurting as of this moment and 9,9-oriented workers get the client to think about what he or she can do, starting at once, to alleviate the dilemma. When doing something "now" helps, then it tends to neutralize whatever happened earlier.

TALK ABOUT BOTH BEHAVIOR AND FEELINGS. Your clients' feelings are important, of course, but 9,9-oriented caseworkers focus on behavior. What is the client actually doing that prolongs the problem? If you do not get your client to act on the problem, having feelings about the dilemma may only serve to excuse it. You may have to do something about your problem to improve your feelings. Otherwise the client's problem may be dealt with more effectively by a psychiatrist or clinical psychologist.

GET CLIENT TO MAKE A VALUE JUDGMENT. Everyone has values. Explore your client's value system; find out what he or she considers important and encourage the client to make a judgment on his or her own behavior. You do not have to decide that this or that action is "good" or "bad" but the client can. If the client says "I just have not done very well on this," that becomes a value judgment for the client that can spur additional problem-solving effort.

NO EXCUSES AND NO PUNISHMENT. Few, if any, excuses should be entertained on behalf of the client. Excuses serve to stall progress. It simply means that all of us, clients and caseworkers alike, should be accountable for what we say we will do but without fear of punishment if we make a mistake.

MAKE A PLAN THAT INVOLVES A GOAL. When you take a 9,9 direction there should be a "flight plan" to keep you on course towards your destination. It does not have to be a rigid one but should provide a clear sense of direction for the client and have a built-in backup if the original plan is not working and must be modified or abandoned.

GET COMMITMENTS. It is the client who makes a commitment if any change is to occur. 9,9-oriented caseworkers urge clients to put forth the necessary effort to accomplish the "flight plan." This provides the occasion for steady and sometimes dramatic success for the client.[12]

One set of practical 9,9 interventions is suggested by Blake and Mouton. You might wish to attempt these kinds of interventions as you enter into the client's situation and try to help him or her.

DISCREPANCY INTERVENTION. This intervention calls attention to some contradiction in the action or attitudes of your client. You may help the client recognize that these contradictions might be one of the principal problem sources: "You told me that you were going to schedule an appointment for your son to see Dr. X but I see that your youngster is still missing school due to illness."

THEORY INTERVENTION. You draw on something you know from the behavioral sciences that enlightens the client and gives the client knowledge for action he or she previously did not have. You can draw on ideas like self-concept, depression, the frustration and aggression hypothesis, cognitive dissonance, functional autonomy or motives, and transactional analysis to explain something to the client: "Some behavior in the teenage years is accounted for by the fact that youngsters have a low self-esteem and are unsure of themselves. Have you any thoughts on this about your daughter?" "Some people doing research say that depression is sometimes explained by a chem-

---

[12]Glasser, op. cit.

ical imbalance. This is something you might want to consider discussing with your doctor."

PROCEDURAL INTERVENTION. This is a critique of efforts undertaken by you and your client that may or may not be aiding problem solving. You sit down and explore what you have tried and what did or did not work, things that were overlooked, and ideas that are timely but have not been attempted: "We have been working together for six months to try and improve your sister's situation using SSI, Medicaid, and food stamp resources. Let's evaluate whether these procedures have helped you and see what other options may now exist."

EXPERIMENTATION INTERVENTION. When you or your client have a hunch, an idea, or a curious new approach that might work, this can be designed as a specific effort and tested to see if it produces positive results: "OK, you seem to think that your mother can be motivated if you take her to this faith healer. Let's give it a try for thirty days and see."

PERSPECTIVE INTERVENTION. These are attempts to provide background, direction, or historical continuity that throw light on present and future decisions that may be made during casework services. You review events of the past six months between you and your clients, see how learning can be enhanced from previous mistakes, and reorder priorities as necessary: "The two of you have tried both individual and group counseling, as well as a trial separation in an effort to keep your marriage together. Let's take a look now at what the results have been."

These kinds of interventions are designed to help your client think and act more confidently with your encouragement and support.

A 9,9-oriented agency is likely to provide the kinds of leadership, innovation, and knowledge about social service programs that an agency with any other Grid orientation may lack. Furthermore, the approach to bringing about change in the 9,9-oriented agency itself is experimental in nature. The experiments are controlled in the sense of trying out new practices and assessing their consequences before rejecting them or introducing change on a broad-spectrum basis via administrative criteria alone.

Another measure of a 9,9-oriented agency is that it becomes the model for other agencies that seek to deal with similar or related problems in other communities and geographic areas. 9,9-type agencies have a higher possibility of being funded by federal or other community resources due to their demonstrated successes.

A 9,9 orientation is not an easy one to embrace because the human assumptions upon which it is based call for the kind of behavior that is relatively uncommon.[13] Looked at another way, a 9,9 orientation expresses the values of sound casework and defines the behavioral skills we must all learn to employ if casework is to fulfill the human goals to which it can contribute.

---

[13]Fromm affirms the proposition that a 9,9 orientation involves the ability to act on one's convictions based upon full commitment, while simultaneously maintaining openness to reservations and doubts regarding the validity of such convictions. He says, "... to tolerate uncertainty about the most important questions with which life confronts us — and yet to have faith in our thought and feeling, inasmuch as they are truly ours..." In this way the closeness of faith in one's capacity to reason in a valid manner is coupled with uncertainty as to the validity of results reached. Fromm, E., op. cit., 1955, p. 180; see also Cleveland, S. E. and R. B. Morton, "Group Behavior and Body Image." *Human Relations,* 15 (1962) pp. 77-85; Crutchfield, R. "Conformity and Character." *American Psychologist,* 10 (1955) pp. 191-198; Anderson, H. H. (Ed.), op. cit., p. 119.

Chapter 8

GRID COMBINATIONS AND 9,9 VERSATILITY

BESIDES the five basic theories of social worker-client relationships already described, additional casework orientations can be identified. These are combinations of the five basic or "pure" theoretical positions. They involve two or more of the Grid approaches already discussed — 9,9; 5,5; 9,1; 1,9; or 1,1 — operating in combination, either simultaneously or successively.

The Grid positions constitute anchorages for identifying and analyzing caseworker attitudes and practices. They are pressures acting on individuals to perform casework in a certain fashion. As suggested in Chapter 2, each of us tends to have a dominant or preferred Grid style. When the dominant approach fails to get results we anticipate we may resort to a "back-up" strategy of some other Grid posture. These Grid styles are not fixed and your casework tactics may follow various mixtures.

Paternalism

If you practice paternalistic casework, you exert close control over the client on one hand and extend much care on the other.[1] This makes for a 9,1 plus 1,9 way of relating to your clients. You encourage your clients to be responsible but do little to delegate autonomy, as a paternalistic caseworker retains tight control in client behavior matters. This is a 9,1 kind of direction. However, it is coupled with 1,9-motivated approval-giving on your part, in order to "motivate" the client. You are generous, kind, and loving towards clients when they do what they are told. Clients soon learn that their social worker is not

[1]The paternalistic role is extensively discussed in Freud, S. *Group Psychology and the Analysis of the Ego.* New York: Liveright, 1949.

happy unless they respond in the appropriate manner. In some instances, this is what "locks in" the client to a paternalistic agency and encourages dependency.

The rewards for compliance may be very appealing to clients: more financial assistance, increased benefits, attractive referral services, to say nothing of personal acceptance. Consistent paternalism makes for obedient clients, who may later erupt with "acting out" behaviors. The reason is that the 9,1 aspect of case management disregards the thinking and capabilities of clients and in the long term generates frustration and resistance. When this resentment is masked to get your approval and love, your clients may appear docile and appreciative. However, the arousal of frustration under conditions of dependency tends to produce hate on the part of the client. Benevolent autocrat is another way of saying paternalist, and a missionary orientation can easily become another variation on the same style.

Wide-Arc Pendulum

Under the wide-arc pendulum approach, either a 9,1 or a 1,9-oriented casework style may be operating but not at the same time.[2] Rather, one follows the other. This pendulum swing can be seen when the caseworker pushes for problem solving in a 9,1-oriented manner and, in doing so, arouses resentments and antagonisms from clients. The caseworker recognizes these negative attitudes and then overcorrects, removing pressures and becoming exaggeratedly interested in his or her client's thoughts, feelings, and attitudes as a person. Problem solving may falter but relationships are again smooth. Failure to see results may induce 9,1 again, and the pendulum swing starts all over.

Sometimes when problems or criticisms strike an agency or a particular program that possibly has taken on 1,9 overtones,

---

[2]A case study demonstrating wide-arc pendulum effects in organizational life is reported by Guest, R. H. *Organizational Change: The Effect of Successful Leadership.* Homewood, Ill.: Dorsey, 1962, pp. 17-38. Another case study that also reveals wide-arc pendulum effects is by Blake, R. R., and J. S. Mouton, *Diary of an OD Man.* Houston: Gulf Publishing Company, 1976. A description of and warning against permitting wide-arc pendulum swings to occur is forwarded by Randall, C. B. *The Folklore of Management.* New York: Mentor, 1962, pp. 66-71.

there are feverish attempts to tighten up services. Food stamp certification is made more stringent as an example of a sort of "crackdown" that occurs on client recipients in various categories of assistance. Cost and waste control measures are launched and everyone is held more accountable. As soon as stability is restored, control eases off and a shift towards a 1,9 orientation occurs. The casework services are viewed by the recipients as cyclical. They are unsure of how to respond under such changing conditions.

"Statistical" 5,5

It is occasionally said of a social worker "It's hard to tell anything exactly about his casework style." He or she fits every position on the Grid at one time or another. The "statistical" 5,5-oriented caseworker employs all five basic styles in dealing with clients.[3] The essential feature is that the caseworker does his or her job according to what is thought to be expected. For example, if a client is slow, the social worker comes to expect that and does not push. If the client is easily upset, the worker comes to expect that and eases up on results and offers praise as encouragement. If another client is falling back on his or her job and nearly losing it, a "statistical" 5,5-oriented caseworker expects that and anticipates that termination is inevitable. If the social worker's instructions are arbitrarily resisted by still another client, the caseworker sees this and backs off. If another client wants to be left alone, the caseworker honors that in a 1,1 fashion. In other words, the "statistical" 5,5-oriented social worker hopscotches all over the Grid according to what the client "wants." By treating each client differently, depending upon the client expectations, the social worker's behavior is inconsistent, yet he or she sees little or no contradiction in the actions, since the common element is in "responding to the client."

A "statistical" 5,5-oriented social worker rationalizes this approach by saying that each person is different and unique and,

---

[3]An approach to negotiation strategies, which is of a statistical 5,5 character, is described by Nierenberg, G. I. *The Art of Negotiating*. New York: Hawthorn Books, Inc., 1968.

therefore, creating relationships with each client that are based on mutual dignity and respect is simply not practical. Lacking a concept of change or development, the "statistical" 5,5-oriented social worker "maneuvers," trying to adjust to whatever is expected within the boundaries of the status quo of each case situation. This moving around the Grid is what produces a "statistical" 5,5 "average" in the end.

The Two-Hat Approach

The two-hat approach is used by social workers who separate concern for individual clients and concern for problem solving by wearing an "agency hat" and a "helping hat" at different times and yet being responsible for both. One hat urges you to observe agency policies, so you counsel your clients on the need to follow accepted routines and to adhere to conventional social values. You stress the rewards your client gains by rule-following behaviors and tend to utilize your role as agency representative in order to solve problems. Another hat prompts you to notice the rigidities, inconsistencies, and unhelpfulness of agency or societal expectations of clients. This induces you to put on your "helping hat," which enables you to overlook, sometimes even to pardon, certain client behaviors because this is what "helps" the most at such times. Concern for the individual gets expressed through going around or even subverting conventional values, which are seen as the "cause" of your client's problems. Caseworkers may or may not like to do these things but feel that agency policies or community expectations force them to wear two hats.

The 9,1-1,1 Cycle

This kind of shift in a caseworker's behavior happens when caseworkers are operating in a 9,1-oriented way primarily due to agency or personal pressures for tight control over what is happening. If the client does not make a 1,1 adjustment to this in order to survive and continues resisting, the caseworker may throw up his or her hands in a 1,1 resignation-type of way by saying, "I've had it with this character. If the client does not cooperate with me, I'll just let this case ride." The client may react to this withdrawal of pressure by doing what is wanted. Then the caseworker takes the renewed effort as hope and reverts to 9,1-oriented behavior, at which time the client reacts negatively again. This cycle pervades their interactions throughout the relationship.

In one respect or another each of these combination theories recognizes the dilemma of solving problems through people. Each tries in some way to handle it. However, compound theories distort the basic issue of integrating people into problem solving in their own behalf. Their underlying limitation is that they never seek to produce real change. They deal only with symptoms. The real solution lies in learning to apply principles of human behavior to involve clients and to integrate individual client goals with the goals of a just society.

9,9-Oriented Versatility

Despite many lines of evidence that a 9,9 orientation is the best way to solve problems with and through clients, a widespread belief exists that, "How you perform casework depends on the situation, on what you are trying to accomplish, and what you're up against." Few words more aptly describe what these caseworkers believe than the term "flexibility." The capacity to substitute one Grid style for another, to shift positions back and forth, and to react differently from client to client are all advocated by many caseworkers.

This is known as situationalism or contingency theory. It is pragmatic: if it seems to work, do it. Flexibility is deemed preferable to the consistent application of any casework style, including 9,9. This rejection of "one best way" of conducting human relationships is equivalent to rejecting the idea that effective behavior is itself based on scientific principles. Scientific inquiry demonstrates principles of behavior that undergird specific events. Many activities in biology, physics, aerodynamics, and nutrition, for example, could not be undertaken without this reliance on principle. By analogy, behavioral science principles lie beneath human conduct, provide guidelines for soundness, and help make behavior predictable.

The growth and development toward effectiveness of administrators, supervisors, caseworkers, and clients can be blocked by violating 9,9-oriented behavioral science principles of participation, conflict resolution, goal setting, critiquing, and so on. The larger expense is in longer-term damage to involvement, morale, and the readiness to persevere in finding valid solutions to important casework problems and, therefore, in diminished problem solving. We are suggesting to social workers that if there is "one best way" to design an aircraft or to increase human longevity, there may be a "best way" to develop casework strengths through a human technology based on scientific principles and applied with versatility to specific social service situations.

The concept of versatility provides a basis for understanding how 9,9 casework can be employed consistently, based on sound principles of behavior, and yet brought into use in creative and constructive ways that are (1) unique to particular case situations; (2) unlikely to generate negative side effects, (3) optimal for problem solving and client care, and (4) stimulating to growth for both caseworker and client. Reliance on behavioral science principles and their implementation through versatile applications is comparable to the relationship between scientific principles in physics and their application to engineering problems. Principles are not violated or disregarded. What changes is their application.

Consider the different casework styles. For example, in the same situation you may approach a difficult, somewhat aggressive, hostile client with a closed 9,1 posture. It seems that the situation calls for firm control with a shift to some other style after order is secured and antagonisms reduced.

If you are 9,9-oriented, however, you know that you and the client need to work together. You proceed as if the client has the ability and desire to figure out his or her problems. You present the client with good information, relieve differences with more information, confront differences openly, arrive at mutual goals, and so on. These principles rely on trust and respect and include "engineering specifics" of behavior, which are verified in social psychology, mental health research, and clinical psychiatry as essential for sound problem solving as in the casework situation.

When viewed in this manner, "versatility" is different from "flexibility." The latter is a reaction to strict and arbitrary rules, as in the Protestant Ethic, which do not square with behavioral science principles and which many people find do not square with their own deeper feelings for a richer life. The result was that the situation itself, as subjectively viewed by the person responsible for it, became the sole criterion for its own management. The only constraint tolerated under the situationalist ethic is that others must not be hurt. What happened was that Protestant Ethic rules became confused with behavioral science principles. The possibility of sound guidelines that can contribute to effectiveness was replaced with the "it all depends" philosophy of subjectivism, "without harm to others."

Versatility suggests that a principled approach requires comprehension of laws of human behavior. The caseworker is challenged to find solutions to problem solving/people dilemmas that are consistent with verified laws of behavior.

What behavioral science principles of participation must be respected to ensure sound social work practice? The following examples are based on evidence from many behavioral science disciplines.[4]

Other things equal, the client's productivity, creativity, and

---

[4]How principles undergird behavior can be seen in the following study of problems that managers identify as of highest priority for solution: These are communication and planning. Yet they are symptomatic of deeper problems that are the more basic barriers to effectiveness. See Blake, R. R. and J. S. Mouton, *Corporate Excellence Through Grid Organization Development*. Houston, Tex.: Gulf Publishing Company, 1968, pp. 3-8. This point of view is also in Argyris, C. and D. A. Schön, *Theory in Practice: Increasing Professional Effectiveness*. San Francisco: Jossey-Bass, 1974, especially in the descriptions of Model II, pp. 85-95; Fleishman, E. A. "Twenty Years of Consideration and Structure." In E. A. Fleishman and J. G. Hunt (Eds.), *Current Developments in the Study of Leadership*. Carbondale: Southern Illinois University Press, 1973, pp. 1-40, particularly p. 37. McGregor, D. *The Human Side of Enterprise*. New York: McGraw-Hill, 1960, pp. 45-57, 59-176; Herzberg, F., B. Mausner, and B. B. Snyderman, *The Motivation to Work,* 2nd ed. New York: John Wiley & Sons, Inc., 1959; Herzberg, F. *The Managerial Choice*. Homewood, Ill.: Dow Jones-Irwin, 1976, pp. 49-101.

The basic literature of psychoanalysis and psychotherapy is consistent with this point of view. A formulation is in Dollard, J. and N. E. Miller, *Personality and Psychotherapy*. New York: McGraw-Hill, 1950, pp. 148-154, 432-434.

mental and physical health are better served when —

1. Informed free choice is the basis for personal action, rather than enforced compliance.
2. Active participation in problem solving and decision making is the basis for growth and development, rather than passively accepting instructions as to what to do, or inactivity reinforced by social isolation.
3. Mutual trust and respect is the basis for sound human relationships, rather than suspiciousness and defensiveness.
4. Open communication gives mutual understanding in contrast with one-way, hidden, or closed communication that increases barriers to understanding.
5. Activities are carried out within a framework of goals and objectives that support self-direction rather than direction from outside.
6. Conflict resolution is by direct problem-solving confrontation, rather than by other ways such as suppression, smoothing, withdrawing, compromising, or manipulation.
7. One is responsible for one's own actions, rather than being responsible to someone else.
8. Critique is used to learn from experience, rather than repeating one's mistakes because experience is not studied.

Behavioral Science Principles of Behavior and Conduct
Evaluated by Grid Style*

Principle	1,1	1,9	5,5	9,1	9,9
Free Choice	clients fend for themselves with insufficient information to exercise informed free choice	action is free, except unpopular actions that might provoke tensions in others are avoided	free choice is muted by conformity pressures which keep clients and caseworker moving together	requirements for compliance eliminate free choice by clients	clients are kept informed and are encouraged to influence outcomes which affect them
Active Participation	clients know what to do	involvement in the social aspects of client-to-caseworker relations is promoted	clients are expected to respect and embrace majority views	obedience from the client rather than active involvement is expected	gaining the involvement, commitment, and creativity is prerequisite to high problem solving and morale
Mutual Trust	lack of respect between caseworker and clients prevails	overly trusting caseworkers give clients free rein	clients in good standing have the caseworker's confidence that they won't make trouble	suspicion that clients will not follow through prevails	confidence is based on demonstrated competence by both caseworkers and clients
Open Communication	factual information is passed faithfully to the clients	communication upward from clients is encouraged but downward flow from the caseworker is dampened to absorb anticipated negative reaction of clients	two-way communication is in line with what is acceptable	communication is one-way, hidden, and closed	open expression of thoughts and feelings is promoted

* Reproduced by permission from R. R. Blake and J. S. Mouton, *Behavioral Science Principles to Increase Effectiveness.* Austin, Texas: Scientific Methods, Inc., 1977

Behavioral Science Principles of Behavior and Conduct
Evaluated by Grid Style *(continued)*

Principle	1,1	1,9	5,5	9,1	9,9
Goals and Objectives	goals are ignored as a source of direction or motivation	the caseworker supports and encourages clients to set goals in line with what is attractive to them	problem-solving targets can be achieved with a reasonable effort	rules are used to pressure problem solving to the requirements decreed by the caseworker	understanding of and agreement with goals and objectives provides for cooperation
Conflict Resolution	neutrality prevails in the presence of disagreement	agreement is sought by supporting the conclusions of others when conflict arises, differences are smoothed over or explained away	when tradition or majority view is unavailable, compromise and accommodation through splitting the difference ensures no one loses	winning one's own position or suppressing disagreement demonstrates mastery over clients	when conflict appears, differences are confronted and resolved
Personal Responsibility	clients take responsibility to the degree they want to	clients are provided whatever responsibility they want, but they are not likely to be held accountable for their actions	clients are expected to accept the status quo and to adjust graciously within it	responsibility for the client is held by the caseworker	client and caseworker are responsible for own activities as well as sharing responsibility for joint activities
Critique	comments regarding the client's actions are rare	compliments for both effort and non-effort related actions over-exaggerate positive features; criticism is withheld if at all possible	tentative suggestions are offered which can be shifted if unacceptable to clients	clients are criticized for not measuring up to the social worker's expectations	critique is used to learn from experience why actions are effective and to learn from them

Figure 5

Chapter 9

THE CLIENT GRID

IN this chapter we focus on the Grid-based behaviors that clients may display during casework interaction and how these behaviors affect the social worker. These behaviors emerge from certain factors that influence a client decision to engage or not to engage in casework processes. What are the factors that act on the client independently of Grid style in any casework situation? They are many and varied, but three stand out. Each is an important consideration in how casework is planned.

Ability to Understand and to Feel

Sometimes clients listen to the social worker with their head and sometimes with their heart. Both are crucial. If the client is unable to understand and feel casework, the individual will not be able to tie informational pieces together. This prevents anticipation of outcomes and therefore, in the solution or the prevention of problems, the client may be handicapped.

Desire

Clients desire things in varying degrees. Their desires are related to practical needs and to the problems being faced. Desire for help may be intense, or it may be completely negative. It may also lie in some neutral position.

Expectations

A third consideration that influences a client reaction is personal expectations of what the casework situation is like. The expectation that casework can help in problem solving may be high or it may be low in the sense that a client sees no possibility of receiving real help.

These three (the ability to understand and feel; desire; and expectations) are key factors in the client's mind. Casework is more effective when all are strong, positive, and valid. The most difficult conditions under which to practice casework are when all factors are negative. The majority of clients are somewhere between these extremes. This is why your effectiveness as a caseworker consists of several aspects. One is in helping the client understand what you are saying in a clear, uncomplicated fashion. Another is in testing whether the client has actual or potential desire for help in clearing away emotional obstacles that may exist. Finally, the client's expectations may be realistic or they may be unrealistic.

These factors combine with each other in various ways. They present the caseworker with a different situation with each and every client. That is why each client is distinctive. The social worker must figure out how each client stands on these factors. What makes casework so challenging is that you must make inferences through the client's Grid style and through your own as well.

In Chapter 1 we sketched the Client Grid and pointed out that the client also brings two concerns to the casework interaction. These concerns are similar to those of the social worker. One concern is for solving his or her problem. Another concern is for the caseworker as a distinctive individual. How the client approaches these dual concerns affects the caseworker's attempts to induce change.

The 9,1-Oriented Client and Social Worker Reactions

This client brings to the casework situation a high desire to solve the problem, but a low concern for the caseworker. Although the client may be prepared to work hard at finding solutions to the problem, he or she does not think that the caseworker matters too much in the search for answers. The client may reject the caseworker's suggestions and distrust the counsel being offered. This means that 9,1-oriented clients hide their real desires from the caseworker and are reluctant to share their thoughts and feelings. They make replies like "forget it," "it doesn't matter," and "leave me alone." They attempt to control most aspects of casework and may readily become hostile when confronted by the caseworker.

How a caseworker reacts to 9,1-oriented clients is influenced by the caseworker's own Grid-based style. 9,1-oriented caseworkers get into a "battle" with the client that can lead to a typical win-lose situation, which results in little or no problem solving. What was supposed to be a "helping" enterprise turns into an adversary proceeding where no change is likely to occur.

A 1,9-oriented caseworker reacts differently. This worker becomes overly sensitive to the abrasions which a 9,1-oriented client can cause. The caseworker responds to client hostility with friendliness and pleasantries, hoping warmth will melt the hostility away, but ultimately retreats with hurt feelings. This caseworker interprets the hostility as rejection of his or her good intentions and efforts.

A 1,1-oriented caseworker lets client negativeness "roll off his back" because he or she generally holds neutral and indifferent views about clients anyway. 1,1-oriented caseworkers do not become emotionally involved with recalcitrant clients and are apt to take a "what's the use" or "who cares" posture about whatever is happening.

A 5,5-oriented social worker will try harder to provide answers in advance of the 9,1-oriented client movements. The social worker is inclined to some semi-defensive tactics like "Yes, but" rebuttals with clients, yet will more often stay on a casework course with tried and true and pat responses, saying "The client is not mad at me; he's mad at the world."

The 9,9-oriented caseworker attempts to give a 9,1-oriented client pertinent information concerning the problem under consideration. The caseworker seeks to stimulate client thinking away from preoccupation with dominance and defensiveness. He or she tries to get the client to engage energy in meaningful talk and to identify the most pressing problem areas. When none of these help resolve the client's antagonisms, the caseworker might say "We are unlikely to be able to make progress until we get at and solve your antagonistic feelings toward me. What's wrong?"

The 1,9-Oriented Client and Social Worker Reactions

A 1,9-oriented client brings to the casework situation a low concern for solving the problem and yet a high concern for the caseworker and for being liked and approved of by the caseworker. The result is that this client displays over-interest in the caseworker's ideas and wishes and seeks to engage in whatever behaviors are thought to be pleasing to the social worker at almost any cost. The 1,9-oriented client is easily persuaded even when the caseworker's ideas may not be the best.

The highly impressionable 1,9-oriented client "bends over backwards" not to offend the caseworker in any manner. He or she complies with caseworker suggestions and sometimes comes to believe that problems are being resolved rather than having to admit that little or no progress is occurring. The client reports small problem-solving gains as if they were important breakthroughs and points to minor insights acquired as if they were the product of the caseworker's great skill in understanding. This client is always grateful and profuse in expressing things to the caseworker.

Furthermore, such efforts are not to manipulate the caseworker, and the client may not even be aware of why he or she is responding by doing everything the caseworker seems to suggest.

Given these kinds of client reactions, a 9,1-oriented caseworker is not then likely to probe for the client's real problems. The worker offers more superficial solutions and social services, preferring instead to move on to efforts with other clients. Believing this client is easily induced to do various things, the caseworker does not spend much time in interviews, home visits, etc., and the client may become disappointed with his or her caseworker, yet is unlikely to say so for fear of rejection.

A 1,9-oriented caseworker experiences mutual delight in and admiration for a 1,9-oriented client. Low concern for problem solving meets low concern for problem solving so the casework interactions become a pleasant social matter unrelated to any serious matter. Warmth and congeniality characterize interviews, with little or no evaluation sessions or discussions about mutual expectations or barriers being encountered, unless to discuss them would bring forth caseworker sympathy, which in turn fosters a sense of warmth and understanding. In the long term this could turn into a successful relationship as the client continues to be generous to a highly pleased caseworker.

The 1,1-oriented caseworker sees this client as one that creates no problems. Rather than accurately interpreting the client's desire to be liked, he or she views the client as operating more out of social protocol. Nevertheless, the worker accurately interprets the client's low desire for problem solving since the client initiates no substantial moves in that direction. The worker is not likely to do so either; thus, a typical laissez-faire condition is created, which is unlikely to generate more than nominal problem solving.

5,5-oriented caseworkers tend to excite positive reactions from 1,9-oriented clients. While the worker might not fully satisfy the client's desire to be liked, he or she probably secures some casework contribution. 1,9-oriented clients prefer to say "yes" and to avoid saying "no" to their caseworker. The 5,5-oriented caseworker's problems may begin if he or she tries to get a major behavioral shift from the client. If, all along, the client is unwilling to make that shift, he or she may still say "yes," even up to the last moment. From that point on, rather than say "no," the client may simply defer making the crucial behavioral change.

A 9,9-oriented caseworker knows that a 1,9-oriented client is easy to influence, so the caseworker will proceed slowly in the casework process and try to secure a deeper understanding of client needs and wants. He or she brings up for discussion unrealistic expectations the client may have and attempts to clarify issues so that the client may gain a deeper awareness of the real stakes in the situation. The difficult point is that a 1,9-oriented client is prepared to listen and agree to whatever information is provided, so the worker needs to test continuously that the client really comprehends what is actually being discussed and is prepared to act on the conclusion eventually reached.

The 1,1-Oriented Client and Social Worker Reactions

Even though not intending to do so, a 1,1-oriented client quickly communicates disinterest in anything except gains that require no effort. The resulting inertia places full weight on the caseworker to carry the load if any movement is to occur.

A 9,1-oriented caseworker facing a 1,1-oriented client pushes hard for his or her own point of view and dominates the interaction to the extent that the client is really subject to being "dominated." The result of this is a one-way casework "dialogue." The caseworker's forcefulness is likely to lead the client into further withdrawal. Sometimes a 9,1-oriented worker may not fully recognize this client detachment and will continue to push for behavioral change long after others might draw the conclusion that any further effort is useless.

The reaction of a 1,9-oriented caseworker is to find mutual interests in terms of which to build a relationship, but to become distressed at the 1,1-oriented client's lack of responsiveness. Finding no mutual interests, the caseworker presents ideas in a disheartened manner, feeling compassion and the desire to help but not anticipating success. The caseworker creates so little persuasiveness or pressure that he or she is unlikely to secure any response.

When a 1,1-oriented client encounters a 1,1-oriented caseworker the result is a literal "zero" kind of casework. The worker asks "Is everything okay?" The client responds with "I guess so." Interviewing ends with a caseworker's "See you next month" kind of parting comment. This is the shortest interview likely to occur.

A 5,5-oriented caseworker is not easily discouraged as he or she tries to keep some interaction alive with a 1,1-oriented client. The caseworker interviews according to a standard set of questions and may secure some half-hearted answers from the client. These may provide the basis for some small gains, but only if the client can see "something" for little or no effort.

The 9,9-oriented caseworker puts knowledge and enthusiasm into the casework effort to see whether some enthusiasm might be sparked to overcome 1,1-oriented client apathy. The worker tries to avoid "yes" or "no" questions as a way of promoting discussion and prompting movement. He or she may try to discover what a client's back-up style might be as a basis for further response. This latter prospect is what sometimes makes a 9,9-oriented caseworker successful, at least to some degree, with a 1,1-oriented client. 1,1-oriented clients are an "Ex" something else on the Grid; they were not born 1,1.

The 5,5-Oriented Client and Social Worker Reactions

The 5,5-oriented client expects to be treated in a diplomatic or nice way. He or she does not want to be challenged to think deeply, preferring problem solution that can be accepted with confidence and that is a more or less conventional answer that requires little change from the status quo. 5,5-oriented clients tend to be norm-based in their thinking and tentative in commitments to the caseworker. This makes it difficult for the caseworker to understand how the client views the total situation and how to penetrate client desires and deeper motivations.

The force and drive of a 9,1-oriented caseworker's approach puts certainty into the tentativeness with which the 5,5-oriented client enters the casework situation. There are two ways in which a 9,1-oriented caseworker may make a negative impact from driving forcefully ahead. One is that he or she may pay insufficient attention to client questions, uncertainties, and status needs. The client may feel tension from this kind of treatment. Even though the caseworker's suggestions may be good, a client who is made even more uncertain does not respond to them in a positive and confident way. A second pitfall is that the worker's ideas may not square with client expectations of what is real help. This is because the caseworker is unlikely to probe in depth to understand the source of a 5,5-oriented client's desires prior to recommending a solution. This produces resistance.

5,5-oriented clients who are tentative and uncertain are likely to ask a lot of questions and have trouble making decisions, even after much discussion. This might discourage a 1,9-oriented caseworker who has made a heavy emotional investment in the client. When this discouragement shows, the client may lose faith in the possibility of solving his or her problem.

However, the caseworker's pleasant attitudes and personal interest in the client are likely to be reassuring. The result may be that the caseworker wins a friend but loses an important behavioral change by the client.

The tendency of a 1,1-oriented caseworker is to answer questions in a mechanical or "turned off" manner, and this does nothing to stir a 5,5-oriented client's interests. The caseworker's lack of vigor and enthusiasm does not inspire sufficient confidence in the caseworker by the client to result in any important influence on the client's behavior.

The 5,5-oriented worker finds a most natural opportunity to exercise influence to at least a small degree when dealing with a 5,5-oriented client. Client and caseworker are tuned to each other. Neither is too intense in understanding, desires, emotional levels, or expectations to trip the balance. They can coexist in partial attainment of both Grid concerns, some progress in solving problems, and some feelings of appreciation in that progress.

A 5,5-oriented client is likely to be responsive to a 9,9-oriented approach because the caseworker relates to the client as a person in a genuine way. This caseworker can provoke the client's readiness to participate and to be involved. Being knowledgeable, the 9,9-oriented caseworker can combine high concerns for both problem-solving capacity and for the individual client to seek solutions. This steers client interests into problem-solving channels. The social worker ferrets out the source of client desires and adds confidence to the client's perception that casework can be helpful.

The 9,9-Oriented Client and Social Worker Reactions

A client with a high concern for solving problems and a high concern for the caseworker's potential capacity and readiness contributes in a way that cuts through unsupported caseworker assertions and emotion-laden attempts to influence him or her. If the caseworker gets off the problem-solving wavelength, the client steers him or her back on course again. A 9,9-oriented client knows that caseworkers have limitations too and does not respond on the basis of partial information or an unsound relationship. The caseworker must be constantly "on his toes" in order to keep a viable casework pace.

The 9,1-oriented caseworker's forceful ways are challenged by a 9,9-oriented client who is likely to ask for data and facts. When challenged, the 9,1-oriented worker's inclination is to convert the objective inquiry into a win/lose argument. This will probably prove to be ineffective because 9,9-oriented clients tend to remain cool. Such a development can ease the worker's approach and help provide factual knowledge in the casework interactions. The attempts to arouse client motivations may meet some success if that knowledge really fits client needs. Thus, if the worker's efforts are in tune with the client's self-formulated requirements, some change on the client's part may occur.

A 1,9-oriented caseworker is likely to feel a lack of progress when dealing with a 9,9-oriented client. The caseworker's lack of in-depth casework knowledge and readiness to glide along on superficial niceties are unlikely to meet the problem-solving requirements of the client and will leave the client unimpressed.

When 1,1 assumptions guide a caseworker's thinking, failure in dealing with a 9,9-oriented client can be anticipated. The worker's superficial style and shallowness of knowledge become evident as the client probes, and this simply does not earn the client's respect.

Because 5,5-oriented caseworkers tend to work from tried-and-true case routines, they are likely to have frequent interruptions in their discussions with 9,9-oriented clients who want clarification and analysis of casework issues, and this may throw them off course. This tests caseworker knowledge and strengths, which might result in more constructive outcomes for the casework process.

The caseworker who is oriented in the 9,9 way finds the greatest personal reward in working with a 9,9-oriented client. The caseworker knows casework and is attuned to both problem solving and a client's individual needs. These match the client's requirements for knowledge and also match his or her method of testing the soundness of possible solutions against what the caseworker offers. The importance of realistic expectations regarding what casework services can or cannot do is equally clear to both worker and client, and both are able to search for valid expectations. These reciprocal attitudes of mutual respect make participation and involvement a natural basis for give-and-take casework dynamics. The caseworker is free to indicate casework help limitations without feeling that he or she is losing a client. It is also possible for the client to accept limitations as realistic when they are unchangeable. The caseworker with a 9,9 approach has the greatest chance of meeting the mind of a 9,9-oriented client in a problem-solving way. The reason is that each person's problem-solving orientation matches the other's. Each of the other social worker/client Grid style combinations lacks one or more of the essential ingredients of problem solving.

Chapter 10

SELF-DEVELOPMENT FOR SOCIAL WORKERS

YOU examined yourself in the Grid Mirror while reading Chapter 2. What you saw then can now be analyzed. Even better, you may want to reexamine the self-description made then and correct it now that you have a more thorough understanding of how the Grid can be used to identify your own social work practice styles.

How did you see yourself? Did you come out predominantly 9,9? Or was it 9,1; 1,9; 1,1 or 5,5? If what you saw was 9,9, is that the real you? Most persons tend to see themselves as 9,9-oriented but careful study of the Grid may show them to be operating otherwise. Research on the Grid, with managers engaged in getting results with and through others, indicates that better Grid understanding and new feedback data leads them to assess themselves more accurately. Can social workers change their Grid orientations if they wish to do so?

Comparison Learning

Learning is essential to change. First we need to know more about conditions that are favorable for learning how to change.

Conditions are favorable for learning whenever a person can make comparisons between two or more things. Then similarities and differences are seen, the reasons for them analyzed, and which of the two or more things is better in terms of relative merit determined. When a person can see similarities and differences, can understand the reasons beneath the surface, and can evaluate them on a "degrees of good and bad" basis, the individual is in a position to plot a course of action for how to get from where one is to where one wants to be.

Let us take this concept of how learning occurs and apply it to changing your Grid style, if this is desirable, or strengthening the one you have, if that is the decision you have reached. First of all, the Grid itself provides the basis for a series of comparisons. In many different ways, as you read this book, you have been comparing 9,9 with 9,1 with 5,5 with 1,9 with 1,1. You can see the similarities between 9,1 and 9,9. One is that both have a high concern for problem solving, but 9,1 disregards the client as a unique and distinctive individual, while 9,9 appreciates the individual as a thinking and feeling person for whom the caseworker should have the utmost respect. That is the key difference.

The 1,9- and 1,1-oriented workers also are similar in that neither has much concern for problem solving. However, a caseworker with a 1,9 attitude enjoys people whereas the 1,1-oriented worker is indifferent to them. So you can see similarities and differences here, too. In the context of all the others, a 5,5-oriented caseworker shares some similarities with them but he or she has very important differences too. In some respects, the 5,5-oriented worker is in the direction of 9,9 but the major difference is that the approach is shallow and conformity-centered rather than deep, committed, and problem-solving centered.

Comparison of Grid Positions

A first step in strengthening your casework is to be clear about the concepts of the Grid. You can test yourself: Take some particular case situation you now have. Write down what the attitude toward that situation would be for a 9,1-oriented caseworker. Then describe the 1,9 attitude. What would be the 1,1 reaction? How would a 5,5-oriented caseworker think about that situation? Finally, picture the 9,9 approach to dealing with it.

Taking your own statements, you might then want to turn to parts of this book related to the same or similar case situations and test your statements against the text. You might want to change some of your answers and to refine others. You may find that writing these statements aids you in diagnosing various ways of seeing a casework situation and therefore in dealing with it. If you do this from time to time, you may find that it continues to strengthen your understanding of the Grid. It can help you in self-diagnosis, because you are able to see ways of dealing with the situation that might differ from your presently characteristic approach.

Compare Your Attitudes with the Grid

You can compare and analyze similarities and differences among these five major orientations, but, of course, there is something far more important if you want to change or strengthen your casework effectiveness. It is to compare your own attitudes with those of the Grid and see which Grid orientation corresponds most directly with your own. This involves searching for similarities between you and each of the five positions. By looking at your rankings in Figure 4, you can determine which Grid style you believe to be most characteristic of yourself by finding the Grid style with the largest total. This will help tell you where you are.

A second step is to come to your own conclusions as to why you are where you are on the Grid and then to decide whether being there is where you want to be. In coming to this conclusion, it is helpful to analyze which of the Grid styles is not at all like you, shown in Figure 4 by the Grid style with the lowest total. This is important because it will tell you something about your aversions. Once you understand what it is you dislike, you may very well want to ask yourself if you act poorly with clients who represent in their Grid styles the Grid style you reject in yourself. This can help you see what it is about some clients that irritates you. You can answer questions for yourself as to how you might work more effectively with clients who represent the things you dislike in yourself.

The chances are that once you understand your own feelings and actions, you will find it possible to be more constructive and positive in working with your clients.

Choosing What Is Ideal for You

There is another way you can use the Grid as the basis for your self-development. It involves identifying the Grid style that fits your ideal self best. This is the one you think to be ideal as the most effective way for you to do casework. Go even further. Identify what is the soundest backup for you to adopt and what situations would impel you to use it. Knowing the Grid description that currently fits your ideal self best and knowing the Grid style that describes your current approach provides one basis for you to set development objectives for yourself. In making this comparison between the actual you and the ideal you, you may be able to see what it is you do that is sound and what it is you do that is not sound. You may also be able to see what it is you do not do that you need to do to act in a truly sound way.

Assume you selected a 9,9 orientation as ideal for you. That is the most likely possibility. No matter how sound any particular Grid style you chose might seem to be, it is realistic for you only insofar as it is workable. 9,9 is a practical and very sound problem-solving approach that most caseworkers are capable of adopting and to which most clients respond favorably. However, there are situations where 9,9, or any style you adopt as the soundest, may seem unworkable because your skill in casework under that situation may be insufficient. The behavior of your client may be such as to obstruct completely your chosen approach in a particular interview. Your soundest casework style may not seem feasible because of some of your agency's policies and practices. In situations such as these you may find yourself slipping into a backup strategy temporarily until you see an opportunity to return to the dominant style that you have found to be the soundest.

Thus, the real test in self-development is learning to increase the skill and versatility with which 9,9 solutions can be implemented so that it will seldom be necessary to adopt backup assumptions. You may also be able to find ways of initiating and taking part in constructive discussion and improvement of your agency's social service programs.

Compare Your Casework Strategies with Other Caseworker's

Let us move into another basis for comparison for a moment. What else can you do for your own self-development? In many situations there are other caseworkers or colleagues of yours who are doing casework. Use the Grid to analyze them in your own mind. What are their strengths and weaknesses? What Grid styles do you see in those who are least effective; what conclusion does this lead you to? Can you see behavior in those who are most effective that is different from your own and that, if you were to adopt it, would give you even more strength? Do you see behavior in the least effective worker that you see in yourself, behavior that you need to change?

There is another thing you can do by reversing the mirror. Give this book to your supervisor or to colleagues, that is, to people who have had a chance to observe you being governed by your present attitudes toward casework. Perhaps they have even watched you perform in case situations. Get them to read it, inviting them to read you somewhere into its pages and to jot down notes where they would put you on the Grid. Then, when you have done this, sit down with them and let them give you their feedback on your Grid style. This is an excellent basis for comparison, because you can then evaluate what they think of you against what you think of yourself. This kind of comparison is particularly important because it gives you another person's point of view. It gets you outside of yourself and opens you up to feedback from others.

Ask Your Spouse

You can also do this kind of data gathering about yourself by giving this book to your spouse, who knows you as well and perhaps better than anyone else. She or he knows what turns you on and what turns you off, what you accept, and what you cannot take. Ask your spouse to read the book and then return to Chapter 2 and pick out paragraphs and elements that are most typical of you. You can gain a great deal of good understanding of yourself through his or her eyes. Incidentally, if you do this, you may find that it has some very good effects on your marriage. Many people have found the Grid a useful way of analyzing how a husband and a wife exert influence on one another and also how both act with regard to their children. This can be very important beyond your interest in casework.

Compare One Client with Another

You have another basis for comparison when you constantly study and compare one client with another. In this way, you get to know your clients in Grid terms so that you can see what it is in them that increases or reduces your own effectiveness. When you see this clearly, you are in a position to work more effectively with the client's Grid style.

In conclusion, you may be well rewarded by comparing, analyzing, evaluating, and drawing conclusions as these relate to what you should or should not do as a basis for your next step in development. This is a truly sound basis for self-development.

Experiment with and Critique Your Casework Styles

Although making comparisons, drawing conclusions, and setting personal objectives are necessary, they are not enough. You must also act upon your self-recommendations and then study the consequences. Did your actions do what you planned for them to do? Did they produce good or bad results? Why? More learning seems to come from critiquing yourself, but you can critique yourself only if you experiment. Design personal experiments; conduct an experiment, evaluate it, and plan next steps.

A good way of doing this is to design experiments so that they, too, provide comparisons. Take, for example, two comparable case situations. Apply your characteristic way in one of them; this is your control condition. Apply your new strategy in the other; this is your experimental condition. Having conducted the experiment, study the results from each. Did the experimental condition produce better or poorer results than the control condition? Why? What is the implication? Was it a poor experiment? Was it a good experiment that failed to give the results you expected? When you can answer these questions, you are in a position to repeat the experiment in order to develop skill in doing the new action in comparison with the old or perhaps in retaining the old practice while combining it with others. Then you can design additional experiments.

Just one word of caution. Think the experiments through. Do them one at a time. Be thorough.

Chapter 11

PAST PRACTICES AND FUTURE TRENDS

CASEWORK is a form of social practice. It has always been very important to social work. Sometime around the mid-1960s it lost some of its luster because large social problems loomed in America that casework did not address effectively. Issues related to delinquency, welfare, poverty, and crime seemed unattended by classical casework. Many writers were quick to suggest that casework was not really interested in such public matters. Casework seemed to decline as social work looked for grander and more politically powerful ways to address burning questions of the day.

Yet individuals continued to show up at social agencies seeking assistance with all kinds of problems. Many of the social workers reading this book have been or are presently engaged in serving precisely these clients. You may call your service counseling, guidance, advice, therapy, or whatever, but you are seeking to render a constructive service helpful to persons with problems they are unable to solve by themselves. In social work, this practice has always been termed casework. It flourished strongly for nearly sixty-five years, starting around 1900, and the disappointments with social work in the 1960s were only a temporary setback for a vital and deeply needed human service.

Historical Perspective

A very short historical journey into casework is necessary for two important reasons: (1) You should be aware that casework declined for two reasons, which perhaps can be avoided in the future, and (2) a "new" perspective on casework, like the Grid, now seems required, which departs from the historically traditional casework culture.

Casework's two "mistakes" lie in its preoccupation with individual psychological problems, which resulted in it developing an extreme dependence on psychiatry to solve such human problems. Casework is about individuals and psychiatry is about human behavior, but casework seemed to become so involved with individual psychological problems that it forgot about the environment. It became so attached to psychiatry that it overlooked ordinary, everyday problem solving. Those of you performing nitty-gritty chores in big public agencies know that psychiatry is interesting and very important, but you also know about food stamps, social security, unemployment benefits, bad housing, and other similar matters that may be outside the client's psychic apparatus and must be managed.

There are several scholarly sources that help document casework's exclusive commitment to an individualistic and psychoanalytic focus. Lubove[1] suggests that casework as practiced in medical settings reinvigorated social work and provided new opportunities to get out of charity organization and child welfare. He cites several reasons why casework was influenced into the individualistic model, and two of these are of interest to us now. The Child Guidance Clinic movement and the positions taken by key social work leaders are important here. William Healy and Augusta Bronner were psychiatrists who spurred the Child Guidance Clinic movement. Healy, who wrote a book called *The Individual Delinquent,*[2] had done considerable work with delinquents in Chicago at the Juvenile Psychopathic Institute between 1909 and 1914. Lubove points out that this text was very popular. Social workers were invited by Healy and Bronner to training sessions at their clinic setting where they accepted referrals from social workers and eventually began to hire caseworkers. By the 1920s social workers had become accustomed to thinking of psychiatry as the answer to personality problems and to all kinds of social and personal deviance. This established casework as the core of social work and deflected attention away from social and cultural environments.

---

[1]Lubove, R. *The Professional Altruist.* Cambridge: Harvard University Press, 1965, pp. 90-113.

[2]Healy, William, *The Individual Delinquent.* Boston: Little Brown and Company, 1915.

Lubove nominates Charlotte Towle and Virginia Robinson as illustrative of what key social work leaders were saying in the late 1920s. Towle explained that "we must meet the basic emotional needs of the individual through the worker-client relationship in terms of parental needs." Those who came for casework help were deemed to have deeply rooted needs to be guided by parental hands. Robinson put forth the conviction that "all social casework, insofar as it is thorough and insofar as it is good casework, is mental hygiene." Casework not founded on this premise "is simply poor casework, superficial in diagnosis, and blind in treatment." The therapeutic relationship had been substituted for solving real problems in living and working.

Lloyd thinks that social workers were not revolutionaries and that despite adoption of social change and reform ideologies, "the predominant emphasis for most social workers remained adjustment, development of inner resources, prevention, and cooperation. The weapon most often used against various forms of social injustice was individual treatment."[3]

A scholarly account of casework theory evolution is offered by Germain,[4] who recounts Mary Richmond's association with Johns Hopkins physicians and medical students and how she came to write about pauperism as a disease and caseworkers as healers. Germain thinks that casework sought to make itself scientific by choosing a medical model of service. She relates to one of the primary concerns of this writing when she claims that an inherent bias in this medical model kept caseworkers "more concerned with the person than with the situation."[5]

Agreement with Lubove, Lloyd, and Germain about the individualistic stance of casework comes from Borenzweig, who examines the issue historically and concludes that casework

---

[3]Lloyd, G. *Charities, Settlements, and Social Work.* New Orleans: Tulane University School of Social Work, 1971.

[4]Germain, C. "Casework and Science: A Historical Encounter." In Roberts, R. and R. Nee (Eds.), *Theories of Social Casework.* Chicago: University of Chicago Press, 1970, pp. 3-32.

[5]Ibid., p. 16.

was thrust into a preoccupation with "the individual psyche."[6] A similar conclusion is supported by Briar[7] who identifies one of the reasons for casework's decline as a "retreat to therapy," which altered the course of its development.

Earlier statements by social work writers attest to the pre-eminence of the individualistic psychological view. In describing professional social work, Esther Lucille Brown maintained that casework was the most highly developed form of social work and that "so completely has the philosophy of casework come to permeate all social work that the concern of social work is the individual."[8] She went on to point out that casework had become so successful as an individualized treatment technique that it was extended to most social agencies. She interpreted an American Association of Schools of Social Work Statement of 1940 on the philosophy of social work, as putting "recognition of an attack upon environmental conditions in second place and stressing the fact of major reliance being placed on treatment of individuals."[9]

The 1960s, however, witnessed considerable debate over the efficacy of the individualistic psychological approach. Part of the upheaval concerning the validity of the individual model is outside of social work. In psychiatry, for example, Szasz[10] questioned the concept of mental illness in a number of books and articles. Others have challenged psychiatric methology,[11] the emphasis on psychiatric treatment,[12] and the results of psychotherapy.[13]

All of this tells us that over-preoccupation with psychiatry and with individual internal problems got casework into some difficulty. The time came when environmental considerations,

---

[6]Borenzweig, H. "Social Work and Psychoanalytic Theory: A Historical Analysis." *Journal of Social Work,* 16(1) (1971) pp. 7-16.

[7]Briar, S. "The Casework Predicament." *Journal of Social Work,* 13(1) (1968) pp. 5-12.

[8]Brown, E. L. *Social Work as a Profession.* New York: Russell Sage Foundation, 1942, p. 183.

[9]Ibid., p. 185.

[10]See, for example, Szasz, T. *Law, Liberty, and Psychiatry.* New York: MacMillan Co., 1963.

[11]Glasser, W. *Reality Therapy.* New York: Harper and Row, 1964.

[12]Jackson, D. D. "Action for Mental Illness — What Kind?" *Stanford Medical Bulletin,* 20(2) (1962) pp. 77-80.

[13]Kiev, A. *Magic, Faith, and Healing.* New York: Free Press of Glencoe, 1964.

such as cultural learning or values, language, and the needs of the community were to receive greater attention from caseworkers. Caseworkers not only have an obligation to serve the individual client per se, but also have an obligation to weigh environmental constraints and the requirements of the community in which the client lives. Social caseworkers and social group workers work directly with individuals, families, and groups in order to assist them to function more effectively in their social environments.[14]

Evolutionary Trends

Given this historical profile of casework, what does the future hold for social workers who wish to sharpen or enrich their practice styles? Changes in social work strategies with individuals parallel broader social changes.

Away from 9,1

Change seems to be away from the raw 9,1 control mechanisms inspired by the hard work ethic, self-control, and the denial of enjoyment in the pursuit of perfection. The 9,1 spirit seems to be less powerful among social work oriented programs, except where the federal government is involved. In this instance, 9,1-oriented federal legislation like equal opportunity, affirmative action, and specific minority designed programs, along with other firm civil rights judicial decisions, will probably rekindle a 9,1 spirit in various ways. Federally funded social service programs that have to comply with governmental guidelines in turn influence the kinds of direct services rendered by social workers. However, in spite of the increased number of social workers operating today, 9,1 practice is probably less evident than was formerly the case.

Toward 1,1

Some factors are driving the evolution of social work in the 1,1 direction, such as machines that result in the simplification

---

[14]Tripoa, T., P. Fellin, I. Epstein, and R. Lind, *Social Workers at Work.* Itasca, Illinois: F. E. Peacock, 1972.

of work and computer serviced agencies that control decision making and eliminate the thinking part of work. However, actual automation, as opposed to mere mechanization, almost always frees people from repetitive, mind-deadening tasks. Many social workers have been freed, through automation, to devote more time to interpersonal relations with clients.

Toward 1,9

At the same time, a welfare society, in the extreme of its development, makes few or no demands and provides approval while asking little effort in return. This seems to constitute a major trend in modern political democracies that exchange votes for welfare security. If this is true, those individuals who carry out the direct service aspects of this philosophy, like social workers, will support the welfare view. They will "champion" or "advocate" for their clients rather than be objective and provide equity. In other words, there is some trend toward a 1,9-oriented client-focused social work practice when clients are seen as oppressed or otherwise dehumanized by the larger society.

Toward 5,5

As a 9,1 orientation becomes less popular, social workers abandon this style while still lacking the skills to shift to 9,9. They choose 5,5 over 1,1 and 1,9, thus creating a strong trend in the 5,5 direction. Forces which culminate in a 5,5 adjustment are powerful and increasing. As agencies grow, they become more bureaucratic. Federal social services dealing with economic opportunity, health care delivery, comprehensive mental health and mental retardation services, etc., have become politically institutionalized. The concepts and procedures of politics influence these social services, and the social work outcome is characterized by compromise, bargaining, and power plays. 5,5 may become the new status quo, the established way, as social work administrations and practitioners seek to get their share of the resources pie.

Schools of social work have become especially vulnerable to federal influences because so many of them are dependent on federally funded educational projects. The majority of these schools have facilities that rely heavily on government monies and receive student financial aid support often for specific enterprises like drug abuse programming, alcoholism, and services to the elderly. Curriculum goals have moved away from training social workers to serving individuals and into preparing students for program planning and larger social system objectives. This "systematic" approach tends to lock students into more bureaucratic processes that emphasize "accountability," "objectives," etc., and provide 5,5-oriented adjustments.

Toward 9,9

There are pressures, however, against 9,1 domination and mastery, 1,1 resignation and abandonment, 1,9 support and approval, or 5,5 accommodation and adjustment. They point toward the 9,9 direction for social work.

Social work education, constantly on the march, provides new insights, skills, and service delivery models. The rise of the minorities, bringing a new cultural awareness, has already influenced social work education and has provided new perspectives on practice.

Casework's shift from individually focused psychopathology in clients to a more holistic view of problem solving is a clear 9,9 thrust. Casework has moved from over-reliance on psychiatry and ego psychology to receiving input from social psychology research and the more specific issues concerning human sexuality, feminism, racism, criminality, and so forth. Caseworkers who focus on a narrow medical model view of behavior are no longer in a majority and will have to face the fact that many clients are experiencing a burden in living rather than mental illness. This calls for new casework goals, alternatives, strategies, and ways of evaluating results that will put caseworkers more onto a 9,9 path.

The search goes on for better ways to perform social work practice than anything known in the past. In addition to a wider application of sociobehavioral science principles, social work is seeing its members receive higher compensation, merit rewards, and greater status. The education of social workers has now leveled off at paraprofessional, baccalaureate, master's, and doctoral plateaus. Each of these levels is making contributions to practice and to implementing new modalities of service to individuals, groups, organizations, and to larger social systems.

Evaluating the strength of these trends in comparison with the others leads us to believe that the 5,5 orientation will continue to rise. It will peak some years ahead when social workers recognize that the erosion of willpower tends to produce adverse consequences. We think that a 9,9 age will come to the social services although attitudes about 9,9 vary. The 9,1 attitude toward it is pessimistic; 5,5 sees it as impractical and idealistic, 1,9 as too demanding, and 1,1 as impossible.

Those who have studied and experimented with 9,9 in different professions and enterprises recognize that it is attainable. They want self-respect that comes from respect for others, be they clients, social workers, or administrators. They want meaningful relationships with the problem-solving and individually centered interests that only mutual respect and common purpose can sustain. The trend toward 9,9 is sound, and social workers are challenged to create conditions so that it can be brought into use on a wider scale.

Chapter 12

HOW SOCIAL WORK SUPERVISORS CAN HELP THEIR SUBORDINATES

SOCIAL work supervisors can assist in the development of the social worker. A few suggestions of how this may be approached are outlined in this chapter. These also constitute important ways in which a supervisor can aid a second-year student in enriching field experience or practicum course.

Reviewing Grid Styles

One of the most difficult things for any person is to make an accurate self-assessment. There are numerous reasons for this. Among the more important is the fact that many people misjudge their good intentions for what they actually do, rationalizing that any difference that exists is necessary by virtue of circumstances encountered in the situation. A person is known by others, of course, for what he or she does, not for the underlying intentions or rationalizations.

Because this self-deception is so widespread, it can be very helpful for you, a social work supervisor, to answer the five Grid paragraphs found in Chapter 2 for each social worker who reports to you. Try to portray how you, the supervisor, see the social worker in his or her dealings with clients. The same ranking procedure is used to picture the subordinate as is outlined in Chapter 2. The only difference is that you are recording your observations about the subordinate rather than using the Grid paragraphs to characterize yourself.

Once this is done, meet with the social worker and compare rankings. It is probable that differences between the two sets of rankings exist. The social worker can review how he or she evaluated him- or herself, and you can review how you evaluated the social worker, with each of you trying to understand the differences in perception. Some of the more likely differences include the following.

One person sees a 9,9 orientation in the top rank position. The other sees 5,5 as the fundamental orientation. When this happens, it is worthwhile to listen to the person whose observation was 5,5-oriented. This is more likely to be the accurate assessment, but it ought to be discussed, using as many examples as necessary to get consensus.

Another distortion is when one person sees a 9,1 orientation, while the other observes a 9,9 orientation. Other things equal, it is preferable to give credibility to the judgment of a 9,1 orientation, as the 9,9-oriented judgment is more likely to be the one involving subjective distortions.

The same line of reasoning should be applied when one person observes his or her own style to be 9,9 while the other person characterizes the individual being pictured as 1,9. In this case, the 1,9 judgment, other things equal, is more likely to be correct.

This exercise between you and the social worker can be greatly enriched if a relationship exists that permits you to reverse this process. The social worker makes rankings to characterize how he or she sees you reacting to clients as well as subordinates, followed by the process described above of discussing the differences between the social worker's perception of you and your self-perception. This is important because the social worker often deals with clients in a manner influenced by how you wish conferences to be handled. If these influences are discussed in an open manner, it can have a positive impact on the social worker's effectiveness with clients. In this way, the sometimes subtle influence of a supervisor's "party line" approach can be examined for validity and objectivity.

Tape Recordings

Another way you can help the development of the social worker is for the social worker to make tape recordings of the client and then to listen to them with you and discuss what is going on. Many clients are quite willing for this to be done, recognizing that social workers are themselves pledged to confidentiality, and that the tapes will only be used for purposes of studying development.

You and the social worker can stop the tapes at points that seem to reveal interesting issues. You can assist the social worker to analyze what his or her assumptions may have been at each of these critical choice points. Additionally, it is important that you help the social worker analyze the client's Grid style and, in this way, possibly help the social worker alter his or her approach. Means of bringing about improvement include instruction in the following areas: (1) aiding the client to gain relief from tensions by expressing anger, (2) assisting the client to lift him- or herself from depression through reinvolvement strategies, or (3) seeing how the client might be assisted to further identify the dilemma that is confronted and exploring alternatives in terms of which these dilemmas might be more constructively approached.

Questionnaires and Other Self-Assessment Instruments

Questionnaires and other self-assessment instruments can aid social workers in examining how they are interacting with their clients and can additionally assist a social worker in constantly studying his or her social work Grid style.[1]

Termination Interviews

Under certain conditions, that is, where there is a genuine motivation for learning from experience, the supervisor can conduct a short critique session with the client after the case is closed. This session is for the purpose of assessing the quality of the relationship and character of problem solving that occurred between client and social worker. This kind of a post-interview is a source of invaluable information to aid a social worker to increase his or her effectiveness. The danger, of course, is that such a procedure either becomes "mechanical" and routine and is of little value or is used as a surveillance device in a punitive way to the detriment of the total agency

[1]For further information contact Scientific Methods, Inc., Box 195, Austin, Texas 78767.

program. Both of these can be avoided, however, and when such post-interviews are carried out in a professional manner, they can provide significant gains not only to the social worker but also to the agency.

The Critical Incident Approach

Another way of strengthening understanding of the Grid and of one's Grid style behavior and conduct is through the social work supervisor and the social worker studying and discussing critical incidents that are already documented in the agency. The purpose is to identify what Grid styles the social worker and client were operating under in these critical incidents. Many such critical incidents are available in agency files, and they are a rich resource for exploring problems that have arisen in the past that, had they been identified at the time, might have been dealt with in a different and better way. Numerous critical incidents are reported in the social work literature. These might also be discussed on a case-by-case basis.

Sometimes such discussions can involve the social workers who report to the same social work supervisor, and this has additional benefits from enriched discussions and strengthened professional norms.

Case Work Conferences

If the professionals in an agency who review active social work cases convene to discuss how the case is being handled and the options and alternatives available to the social worker for dealing with each of the particular cases, these discussions can also be enriched by examining the client's and social worker's Grid styles. Exploring with the social worker who is responsible for each case alternative ways by which he or she might deal with the client to increase a problem-solving attitude is one possible beginning. Once social workers have a grasp of the Grid framework and feel comfortable with using the language of the Grid in identifying and discussing problems, the arena of issues that are open for discussion becomes substantial.

Role Playing

Sometimes insight and clarification regarding a social worker/client dilemma can be achieved through the various techniques of role playing. For example, one social worker can take the role of the client, and the other social worker plays his or her own "typical" role in the discussion, enacting episodes of discussion. The role playing director may interrupt the flow of conversation at critical points in order to bring the attention of the participants and the audience to bear on various facets of the episode. Role reversal can then occur, or another social worker may replace the designated social worker in order for the designated social worker to see how someone else might deal with the same problem, etc. Among the unusual benefits of this approach is that, when a problem has been uncovered in the social worker/client interaction, the social worker can rehearse alternative actions that might be given consideration for dealing more appropriately with the client's problem. Confidence can be gained in this way as to the feasibility of altering his or her approach in the next client contact.

Social Worker Grid Seminars

Scientifically designed Social Worker Grid Seminars, engineered to provide the social worker with an intensive interaction experience in solving social worker problems with other social workers, are also available for use in development. The individual social worker can attend publicly conducted programs, or the agency can conduct its own Social Worker Grid Seminar on an in-house basis.

These seminars are several days in length. They offer the social worker a "total" experience, actively participating with others in seeking solutions to problems under circumstances where each participant, in a thousand different ways, reveals his or her Grid style. Part of the activity involves comprehensive feedback to each participant from other team members as to what they have observed in his or her social worker attitudes and behavior from a Grid perspective.

These seminars are rewarding and have a significant impact

on change in terms of increasing social worker effectiveness. When conducted on a within-agency basis, they do much to strengthen the organization's professional culture by bringing stronger values into existence as to how best to utilize the agency's resources for helping clients.

Summary

By using the Grid as the basis for studying critical incidents, role playing, offering the social worker direct feedback, supervisory discussions, and organized educational inputs, the social work supervisor is in an excellent position to assist the front-line social worker's development.

This approach to development can do much to reinforce the self-development activites identified in Chapter 11. Coupled with top level agency leadership, these activities can provide the basis for bringing excellence of professional service into the agency.

Appendix

USE OF THE GRID TO ANALYZE BEHAVIORAL SCIENCE APPROACHES TO HUMAN RELATIONSHIPS*

THE original use of the Grid to analyze interactions between significant variables of management — production and people — occurred in our efforts as consultants to understand a basic conflict in a top management group. One faction maintained that "If we don't put the pressure on for higher production we're going to sink." The other faction said "We must ease up on the pressure and start treating people in a nicer way." Thus, a 9,1 orientation met a 1,9 orientation. This either production *or* people way of conceiving the problem eliminated perception of other possibilities such as getting people involved in the importance of being more productive.

By treating these variables of production and people as independent yet interacting, we came to see many alternative ways of managing: not only 9,1 and 1,9 but also 1,1, 5,5, 9,9, paternalism, counterbalancing, two-hat, statistical 5,5, and facades.

A way of thinking about human relationships that permitted such clear comprehension and comparison of alternatives led us to believe this formulation to be of general significance for understanding other human relationships. Thus we evaluated in greater detail how others had tried to deal with the same kind of question.

We found no systematic use of a two-dimensional geometric space as the foundation for conceptual analysis of assumptions about how to manage, but we were struck by the extent to which such a basis of analysis was being used, either implicitly or statistically. Theorists who used two variables *implicitly*, and without identification of the variables involved, included Horney and Fromm. Other theorists who approached the sit-

---

*Blake, R. R. and J. S. Mouton, *The New Managerial Grid*. Houston: Gulf Publishing Company, 1978, pp. 218-231.

uation *statistically,* without explicit analysis of how assumptions and therefore behavior may change as a function of the character of the interaction of these variables, included Likert and Fleishman.

The table shows the various implicit or statistical approaches for comprehending human relationships that can be fitted into a Grid framework. Several explicit efforts to modify the Grid also are included and are commented on later.

As shown in the table, regardless of their field of specialization, and with but a few exceptions, all investigators describe behavior as if relying on a two-dimensional framework. Factor analytic approaches reinforce conceptual analysis and lead to the conclusion that most meaningful variance in behavior can be accounted for by two factors.

There are exceptions, however. One is Bales, who described behavior in a three-variable geometric space, the third variable being related to an individual's acceptance or rejection of conventional authority. The added complexity did little by way of extending understanding of behavior. Another, by Schutz, added *inclusion* as a third dimension, but little use has been made of it in experimental, clinical, or applied work. Reddin and Hersey and Blanchard have added effectiveness as a third Grid dimension, but this is not a true third dimension since effectiveness is already determined by the first two and therefore is not independent of them.

There is an implicit third dimension within the Grid framework, however. It involves identification of motivation as a bipolar scale, ranging, in the 9,1 case for example, between control, mastery, and domination on the plus end to dread of failure on the minus end of the scale. While adding a third dimension of motivation introduces further clarification as to what a 9,1 or other Grid orientation is like, little in predictive utility for understanding everyday behavior is gained over that already available in a two-dimensional system. This motivation dimension is available elsewhere and is not further dealt with in this context.

A further comment of importance in understanding the Grid is the concept of *interaction.* Interaction between these variables can occur in either of two ways. The combination of any two quantities can occur in an arithmetic way. This needs to be distinguished from the fusion of two quantities in a "chemical" way. Hersey and Blanchard, for example, might see 9,9 as a combination of 9 units of task orientation, telling a subordinate in great detail "who, what, where, and how . . ." added to 9 units of relationships, involving extensive compliments and appreciation expressed in response to subordinate compliance. The "chemical" view, by comparison, produces a 9,9 character of interdependence in which shared participation, involvement, and commitment produce consensus-based teamwork. In the former case, combination of variables is quantitative and arithmetic; in the latter, it is qualitative and organic, i.e. the *character* of the behavior itself changes, not just relative to the amounts of the same behavior.

Because most investigations have found a two-dimensional basis sufficient and three-dimensional formulations have added little to understanding beyond that already available from the use of two, we conclude that a framework for analyzing behavior that results from two variables is a sound and sufficient basis for comprehending assumptions and practices.

Catalog of Approaches to Human Relationships Through a Grid Framework

Investigator	Source	Field	9,1	1,9	1,1	5,5	9,9	Statistical 5,5	Facades	Pater-nalism	Other
Argyris, C.	*Management and Organizational Development: The Path from XA to YB.* New York: McGraw-Hill, 1971.	Organization Behavior	xi, xii, 6-15,66-70. 73-74, 77-78, 85-88 105, 107, 134, 135, 138-140			13-14, 30-34, 56-57	xi, 15-20,21-22,24 42,57-61, 67-70, 85-89		19	3,62	
Argyris, C. & Schon, D.A.	*Theory in Practice: Increasing Professional Effectiveness.* San Francisco: Jossey-Bass, 1974.	Business Administration	66-84 101-102, 104, 105-106, 107-108, 149-155				85-95, 101, 102-104, 105, 106-107, 108-109				
Arkava, M.L.	*Behavior Modification: A Procedural Guide for Social Workers.* Missoula: U of Montana, 1974	Social Work	16-66					1-11		1-82	
Bach, G.R. & Wyden, P.	*The Intimate Enemy.* New York: William Morrow and Company, Inc., 1969.	Psychology	8-9, 45-46,48-49, 71-73,75, 83,109-117,129, 141-150, 256-257, 311,312, 314	5,48,71-73,84-85, 97,102-108,311, 314,321-322	31-32, 312	5, 53-54 135-136	36,43 53,91 119-123, 137,161-165,257-258,343-348		7,10,13, 19,36, 103,120, 159,196-197,222-223,253-254	113	Sick 9,1 112-113, 151,158, 160,260 Distorted 1,9:75, 112,154, 158,160, 260,331 Change 173-174
Bales, R.F.	*Personality and Interpersonal Behavior.* New York: Holt, Rinehart & Winston, 1970.	Sociology	193-199, 213-219, 220-229, 230-237,	200-207, 252-257, 313-319, 320-326, 369-376	289-296, 332,339, 340-346, 347-353, 354-360, 361-368, 377-386	191, 258-264, 265-272, 327-331	208-212	190, 273-281,			Balance 5,5:191 Machiavellianism 238-241

Investigator	Source	Field	9,1	1,9	1,1	5,5	9,9	Statistical 5,5	Facades	Pater-nalism	Other
Barber, J.D.	*The Presidential Character:* Englewood Cliffs, N.J.: Prentice-Hall, 1972.	Applied Politics Political Science	12-13,17-57,58-98, 99-142, 347-395, 413-442, 446-448	13,91, 173-206, 448-450	13,145-163,165, 166-167	170-173	12, 209-343, 452-454	79,86, 92-93	83	60,91	Two Hat: 86,87 Critique: 277-278, 331
Bell, G.D.	*The Achievers.* Chapel Hill, N.C.: Preston-Hill, Inc., 1973.	Business	23-38, 39-59, 132-152	73-83, 164-171	60-72, 153-163		104-124, 181-187		84-103, 172-180, 188-195		
Benne, K.D. & Sheats, P.	"Functional Roles of Group Members." *Journal of Social Issues 4,* no. 2 (1948): 41-49.	Clinical Psychology	45,46	44,45, 46	45	44	44		46		
Bennett, D.	*TA and the Manager.* New York: AMACON, 1976.	Business Consultant	14,19,26-27,30-32, 122,145 146-150, 161-162, 164-165, 230	14,26-27,32, 122,160-161,168-170,230-231	79,80, 145, 153,154, 160-161	18-19, 79-82, 129-137, 145,150-153	26-27, 81,82, 83,139-140,145, 154-157, 178,194-196,230		81,82, 91-116	231	Dom/Backup: 151-152, 181 Wide Arc: 230
Berne, E.	*Games People Play.* New York: Grove Press, 1964.	Psychiatry	27,112, 113	25-26			27, 178-179, 180-181, 182-183, 184		48-168		
Biestek, F.P.	*The Casework Relationship.* Chicago: Loyola U Press, 1957	Social Work	106- 107	33- 47	108	48- 66	67- 99, 100- 119	23 -32			
Bion, W.R.	*Experiences in Groups.* New York: Basic Books, 1959.	Psychoanalysis	152-153	147-150	152-153	150-152	156-158, 169				Dom/Backup: 160-165
Blake, R.R. & Mouton, J.S.	*The Grid for Sales Excellence: Benchmarks for Effective Salesmanship.* New York: McGraw-Hill, 1970.	Social Psychology	45-58	59-69	70-79	80-94	95-118	187	125-136	188	Dom/Backup: 13-15
Blake, R.R. & Mouton, J.S.	*The Grid for Supervisory Effectiveness.* Austin: Scientific Methods, Inc., 1975.	Social Psychology	11-28	29-43	44-58	59-78	79-107				Dom/Backup: 8-9

Investigator	Source	Field	9,1	1,9	1,1	5,5	9,9	Statistical 5,5	Facades	Pater-nalism	Other
Branden, N.	*The Psychology of Self-Esteem.* New York: Bantam Books, 1969.	Psychiatry	188-190	150,151	194-195	185-188	109-139, 146				
Burns, T. & Stalker, G.M.	*The Management of Innovation.* New York: Barnes & Noble, Social Science Paperbacks, 1961.	Organization Behavior	96-125				96-125				
Buzzotta, V.R., Lefton, R.E., Sherberg, M.	*Effective Selling Through Psychology: Dimensional Sales and Sales Management Strategies.* New York: Wiley Interscience, 1972.	Clinical Psychology	36-53 99-100a, 120-121, 127,264-270,285-286,301-318,319, 320-324, 338-339, 344-347, 357-358, 358-359	68-82, 99-100a, 122,124, 127,274-277,287-288,301-318,319, 327-331, 340-341, 344-347, 358,359	54-67, 99-100a, 121,122, 127,270-274,286-287,301-318,319, 324,327, 339-340, 344-347, 358,359		83,98, 99-100a, 124,125, 127,199-224,277-283,288-289,301-318,319, 331-334, 341-343, 344-347, 358,359-360		113-117, 291-292		Dom/Backup: 101-112, 289-291
Durkheim, E.	"On Anomie." In C.W. Mills, ed., *Images of Man: The Classic Tradition in Sociological Thinking.* New York: George Braziller, Inc., 1960, pp. 449-485.	Sociology	455-461	460	460-461	449-461					

Investigator	Source	Field	9,1	1,9	1,1	5,5	9,9	Statistical 5,5	Facades	Paternalism	Other
Etzioni, A.	*A Comparative Analysis of Complex Organizations,* (Rev. ed.). New York: Free Press, 1975.	Sociology	xxiv,5-6, 8,12,15 27-31,56-59,60-61, 66-67,75-82,84,106, 115,116-118,133, 287,455-460,471, 479,486-490,500-504		28,289	xxiv,5-6 6-8,12, 15,40-54, 56-59,61-72,78,81-82,89,92, 106,114-117,169, 305-311, 426-427, 455-460, 471,479 486-490 500-504	471	433-436, 437-438		xxiv,5, 6-8,12, 15,31-39, 62-67,72-75,78-82, 84-87,89, 106,112-113,116, 271,389-391,426-427,455-460,471, 479,486-490,500-504	Machiavellianism: 387
Fleishman, E.A.	"Twenty Years of Consideration and Structure." In E.A. Fleishman and J.G. Hunt, eds., *Current Developments in the Study of Leadership.* Carbondale: Southern Illinois University Press, 1973, pp. 1-40.	Industrial Psychology	25-26, 26-27, 29,32	23,25, 26-27, 29	26-27, 29,32, 36,37	29	23-24, 24-25, 26-27, 27-29, 32,35, 37	37			
Fromm, E.	*The Art of Loving.* London: Unwin Books, 1957.	Psychiatry	23,25, 31,43, 54-55	9,23,25, 42-43, 55-56	15-16, 23,83-84	10-11, 18-22, 25,74-76,80	24,26-28,29, 42,53-54,87, 104-109			82-83	
Gordon, T.	*Parent Effectiveness Training.* New York: Peter H. Wyden, 1970.	Counseling Psychology	10-11,41-44,83-86, 110,112-113,151, 152,153-159,174-183,195, 207,248, 260-261, 263,280, 321-322, 323-324, 325,326-327	11,13-14, 43-44, 151,152, 154-155, 159-161, 184,190-193,248, 251-253, 324-325, 326	44,152, 183,185, 327	42-43, 110,113, 184,289, 322,323, 324,325-326,327,	12,30-31,33, 47-61, 194-264, 280-282, 305-306	261-263	22-25	11,166, 168-169, 177-178, 190-191	Wide Arc: 11,161-163

Investigator	Source	Field	9,1	1,9	1,1	5,5	9,9	Statistical 5,5	Facades	Pater-nalism	Other
Gordon, T.	*T.E.T.: Teacher Effectiveness Training.* New York: Peter H. Wyden, 1974.	Counseling Psychology	27-29,48-49,80-84, 84-85,86-87,184-185,186-189,191, 192-194, 198-206, 211-216	49,85-86, 184,186-188,189-190,191, 206-207	49,87, 206-207, 208-209	208	220-282			194-195, 213	Dom/Backup: 23-24 Wide Arc: 190-191
Hardman, D.G.	*Authority Monograph.* National Council on Crime & Delinquency	Social Work	219, 245, 246, 248	215-217, 219,249			249-255, 245-254	217, 221, 247, 249-255			
Harrington, A.	*The Immortalist.* Millbrae, Calif: Celestial Arts, 1977.	Philosophy	114,117, 118,119, 123-127, 137,139		117,118, 129-130	100-101, 114-115, 117,118, 127-129	136-139		144-145	120-121	
Harris, T.A.	*I'm OK—You're OK.* New York: Avon, 1969.	Psychiatry	72-73, 263	67-69	69-71, 142-143, 152	143-146, 153	74-77, 151-152, 153,302-304		75-76, 146-151, 152,262-263		
Heath, R.	*The Reasonable Adventure:* Pittsburgh: The University of Pittsburgh Press, 1964.	Clinical Psychology	ix-x, xii 5-6,20-24,38,39 63-67	28-29		ix,xi,4-5,10-11, 14-20,37-38,39, 57-63	ix,x,7, 8-10, 30-36, 39	x,xii-xiii,6-7,24-28, 38,39, 67-69			
Hersey, P. & Blanchard, K.H.	*Management and Organizational Behavior: Utilizing Human Resources.* (2nd ed.). Englewood Cliffs, N.J.: Prentice-Hall, 1972.	Education	35-37,46-48,61,63, 70-76,92-93	61,63, 74-76	70-76	74-76	46-48, 61,63, 70-76	83-86, 121-123, 127-131		61,63, 133-143	Machiavellianism: 92-93 Wide Arc: 125 Change: 149-171

Investigator	Source	Field	9,1	1,9	1,1	5,5	9,9	Statistical 5,5	Facades	Paternalism	Other
Horney, K.	*Neurosis and Human Growth.* New York: W.W. Norton & Co., 1950.	Psychoanalysis	17-39,76, 97,191-213,214-215,304-306,311-316	76-77,97-98,215-238,239-243,316-324	43-44,77-78,259-290,304, 324-328			312-315			Dom/Backup: 232-234 Sick 9,1: 247-256 Distorted 1,9:243-256
Horney, K.	*The Neurotic Personality of Our Time.* New York: W.W. Norton & Co., 1937.	Psychoanalysis	39,81-82, 98,162-187	36,85-87, 96-98, 102-161	99,191-192,212-213,237	28,96-97	104,107, 108,109, 113,163, 273-274	100-101			Distorted 1,9:259-280
Horney, K.	*Self-Analysis.* New York: W.W. Norton & Co., 1942.	Psychoanalysis	44,47-48, 56-57, 57-58, 58-59	54-55	48-52, 55-56, 57,58, 59-60, 62,108	58,108					Wide Arc: 44
James, M.	*The OK Boss.* Reading, Mass.: Addison-Wesley, 1975.	Adult Education	10-11,16-17,20-21, 35,36,39, 40,54,55, 56,57,59, 61,62,75, 76,77, 131,139,	13, 18-19,37, 39-40,75	14-15, 35,55, 56,57-58,59-61,62, 75-76, 135, 139-140	19,37, 77,132, 144	17,21, 54,55, 56,57, 59,61, 62,69, 76-77, 132-133, 139, 144-145, 161-163	27,38,64,	106-121, 124-127	12-13, 35,36, 39,73-75	Dom/Backup: 8-9
James, M. & Jongeward, D.	*Born To Win: Transactional Analysis with Gestalt Experiments.* Reading, Mass.: Addison-Wesley, 1971.	Education	18,36,68-100,101-126,230	18,37, 127-159, 230-231	37,50, 56-57	18,57-58, 58-59, 224-226	18,36, 56-62, 235-238, 263-274	2-3, 227-228	29-35, 58	86, 229-230	
Jennings, E.E.	*The Executive: Autocrat, Bureaucrat, Democrat.* New York: Harper & Row, 1962.	Business Education	2,4,20-21,25,66-70,75-77, 83-86,86-90,114-163			2,4,90-91,91-97, 105-106, 164-195, 228-232	2-3,4, 59-61, 97-106, 196-234	77-80, 256-266	85,250	25-26, 149, 157-160	Dom/Backup: 117
Jung, C.G.	*Psychological Types.* Princeton: Princeton University Press, 1971.	Psychiatry	346-354, 383-387		385-386, 388-391, 395-398, 401-403, 403-405	334-335, 354-355, 356-359, 363-366		368-370	384		Dom/Backup: 355-356, 362-363, 405-407

Investigator	Source	Field	9,1	1,9	1,1	5,5	9,9	Statistical 5,5	Facades	Pater-nalism	Other
Kangas, J.A. & Solomon, G.H.	*The Psychology of Strength.* Englewood Cliffs, N.J.: Prentice-Hall, 1975.	Psychology	7-9,10-11, 14,15-17, 55-56, 56-57, 135-136	18-19,22, 24,78	20-21, 21-22, 23	11-12, 19, 57-58	3,9,12, 21,23-24,24-25,68-69,117, 130-135, 136-141, 142-145, 146-150, 151-168	26-27	13-14,17-18,19-20, 24-25,29-30,56,77		Wide Arc: 136
Kovar, L.C.	*Faces of the Adolescent Girl.* Englewood Cliffs, N.J.: Prentice-Hall, 1968.	Adolescent Psychology	11-12, 73-83, 103-106	9-10, 53-68	79	10-11, 35-51, 83, 148-149	4-9, 107-125, 148-149				
Kunkel, F.M. & Dickerson, R.E.	*How Character Develops: A Psychological Interpretation.* New York: Charles Scribner & Sons, 1946.	Psychology	68-81	60-67	80-82		125-140, 157-159, 176-178				
Leary, T.	*Interpersonal Diagnosis of Personality.* New York: Ronald Press, 1957.	Clinical Psychology	19,64-65, 104,105, 135,137, 233,269-281,324-331,332-340	64-65, 104,105, 135,233, 292-302, 303-314	19,23-24, 64-65,95-96,104, 105,135, 233,282-291	19,64-65, 135,202-203,233, 315-322	21,64-65, 135,233, 323-324		181-186, 188-191, 282-283, 284-285, 316,317, 318,324, 325,326	64-65, 93	Dom/Backup: 225-227 Distorted 1,9:284-286,288-289,367 Sick 9.1: 341-350, 364,372
Likert, R.	*The Human Organization: Its Management and Value.* New York: McGraw-Hill, 1967.	Organization Behavior	3-12, 13-46			3-12, 13-46	3-12, 13-46, 47-100			3-12, 13-46	

Investigator	Source	Field	9,1	1,9	1,1	5,5	9,9	Statistical 5,5	Facades	Pater-nalism	Other
Likert, R. & Likert, J.G.	*New Ways of Managing Conflict.* New York: McGraw-Hill, 1976.	Organization Behavior	19-40, 59-69			19-40	16-17, 19-40, 49-51, 51-56, 71-324			19-40	
McClelland, D.C.	*Power: The Inner Experience.* New York: Irvington Publishers, 1975.	Individual Psychology	7-8,8-12, 13-21,27, 49-51,52-76,77-78, 249,252-254,255-256,257, 258,260-261,264, 266,274-275,295-297-324, 326,328	27,104-122,255, 264,274, 289,322-323,325, 328		27,155, 157-158, 249	27,257, 258,260-261,261-263,263-266,269, 288,301-302,324, 325,329		301-302	35-36, 142-144, 260,289-290	Distorted 1,9:102, 104 Sick 9,1: 255 OD:254, 255
McGregor, D.	*The Human Side of Enterprise.* New York: McGraw-Hill, 1960.	Psychology	33-43				45-57, 61-246				
McGregor, D.	*The Professional Manager.* New York: McGraw-Hill, 1967.	Psychology	59-63, 79-80, 117-118, 118-125, 136-137, 138-140, 148-149	59-63	59-63	59-63, 144-145	29-30, 59-63, 79-80, 118,127-130,130-133,140, 162-182, 191-195			7-10, · 142-144	Dom/Backup: 60
Maccoby, M.	*The Gamesman.* New York: Simon & Schuster, 1976.	Psychiatry	34,47-48, 76-85, 181-182, 183-184, 187-189, 212-213	183-187	94	34,35, 46-47, 48,50-75,86-97,189-209	179,212, 213-217	100,149	48-49, 91,92-93,98-120,121-171	240-241	

Investigator	Source	Field	9,1	1,9	1,1	5,5	9,9	Statistical 5,5	Facades	Pater-nalism	Other
May, R.	*Love and Will.* New York: W.W. Norton & Co., 1969.	Clinical Psychology	45-48, 57-59, 276-278	278-279	27-33	40-45, 279	55-56, 91-92, 146,283-286,303-304,306, 310-311				
Meininger, J.	*Success Through Transactional Analysis.* New York: New American Library, 1973.	Business Consultant	26-27, 28-29, 33,39-40,43-44,64-67,73-75,87-90,128-129	29-30, 34-36, 38,43-44,45-46,67-71,75-76,90-92,105-106,166-170,186-190	36,39-40,40-42,43-44,56-57,100-101,105-106,110-113,153, 157	30-31, 57-60, 76-77	26-27, 36-37, 63-64, 101,113-114,129-130,158-160,165-166,175-177,178-185,186-206	66	7-10,60-63,78-99, 106-109, 173-175	153, 160-161	Wide Arc: 66 Change: 132-139, 194-204
Metcalf, H.C. & Urwick, L.	*Dynamic Administration: The Collected Papers of Mary Parker Follett:* New York: Harper & Bros., 1940.	Government and Administration	31,50-58, 96-101, 272-277			31-32,35, 210-213, 239	31, 33-49, 58-70, 111-116, 198-202		213-225, 240-246, 260-269, 279-281		
Missildine, W.H.	*Your Inner Child of the Past.* New York: Simon & Schuster, 1963.	Psychiatry	77,85-100,103, 106,108-109,125-126-130-133,138-139	77,133-136,157, 166,171-191,259-260,266-267,271-272	78-79, 101-103, 104-105, 107-108, 109-111, 121-124, 145-155, 156-159, 165-166, 166-167, 243-252, 254-259, 261						

Investigator	Source	Field	9,1	1,9	1,1	5,5	9,9	Statistical 5,5	Facades	Pater-nalism	Other
Missildine, W.H. & Galton, L.	*Your Inner Conflicts—How to Solve Them.* New York: Simon & Schuster, 1974.	Psychiatry	35-36,37, 38-39,39-40,62,72-74,76,77, 81-82, 83-86, 131-133, 145-146, 154-155, 171-172, 172-180, 187-191, 196-201, 205-207	36,37-38,61, 76-77, 130	37,39, 53-59, 60,60-61,62, 62-63, 77, 120-127, 157-160, 162-163, 184-187		33-34, 262-263, 308-313				
Moment, D. & Zaleznik, A.	*Role Development and Interpersonal Competence.* Boston: Harvard University Press, 1963.	Business Administration	20,38,56, 62-63,67, 72,77,80, 85-86,87-88,89, 104-105, 122-123, 158-159, 160	20,39, 56,62-63,67, 72,77, 78-79, 80,83, 86-87, 89, 105-106, 123-124, 159-160	20,36-37,39, 56,62-63,67, 72,80, 83,87, 89-90, 106-107, 124-125		19-20, 36-37, 38,41, 53,56, 62-63, 68,72, 77,80, 85,89, 104, 120-122				
Mouton, J.S. & Blake, R.R.	*The Marriage Grid.* New York: McGraw-Hill, 1971.	Social Psychology	41-67	97-113	123-137	151-169	181-201	80-85	76-80	69-74	Dom/Backup: 15-17
Reddin, W.J.	*Managerial Effectiveness 3-D.* New York: McGraw-Hill, 1970.	Business Administration	27,28-29, 31-32,42, 47,73-74, 94-95, 161,177, 192,194, 194-195, 221-227, 262,263, 268-269	27,28-29, 31,42,68, 73,94, 194,215-219	43,48, 54,194, 209-212, 258-259, 263,264,	27,28-29, 30-31,41, 42-43,48, 72-73, 93-94, 194,205-209,213, 231-233	27,28-29,32, 41,48, 74-75, 94,95, 192,194, 230-231, 233-234	52,53-54, 139-140, 149-150, 159-160, 169-178, 181-185, 256-257		42,47	Dom/Backup: 46-47,48, 49,152 Change: 163,307
Reid, W. & Epstein, L.	*Task-Centered Casework.* New York: Columbia U Press, 1972.	Social Work		155-156		136-138	1-260				

Investigator	Source	Field	9,1	1,9	1,1	5,5	9,9	Statistical 5,5	Facades	Pater-nalism	Other
Riesman, D., Glazer, N., & Denney, R.	*The Lonely Crowd.* Garden City, N.Y.: Doubleday & Co., 1953.	Sociology Political Science Economic History	23,28-32, 41,57-63		278,281	23,24-28, 33,34-40, 41-42, 63-74, 278	33,278, 282,286-298,328		302-305, 305-307	303	
Roberts, R.W. & Nee, R.H.	*Theories of Social Casework.* Chicago: U of Chicago Press, 1970	Social Work	181-218	33-75, 131-179			77-128, 313-351				
Schutz, W.C.	*The Interpersonal Underworld* (originally titled *FIRO: A Three Dimensional Theory of Interpersonal Behavior).* Palo Alto, Calif.: Science & Behavior Books, 1966.	Psychology	29,41,46, 47-48,89	31,36,41, 47,48,89	25-26, 28-29, 30-31, 41,42, 45-46, 47,48, 89	26-27	27,29-30,31, 37,41, 43,48, 87-89			43	Sick 9,1: 43 Distorted 1,9:42-43
Steiner, C.M.	*Scripts People Live: Transactional Analysis of Life Scripts.* New York: Bantam Books, 1974.	Therapy	53,54-46, 78-81, 115-119, 188-193, 197-198, 231-234, 236-237, 253-261	54,56, 76-78, 198-201, 211-213, 222-224	92-95, 115-119, 178-181, 218-220, 243-245		3,85-86, 352-361, 362-370, 382-383, 384		44-50, 121, 175-178, 304-305		Wide Arc: 39 Dom/Backup: 37-38

Investigator	Source	Field	9,1	1,9	1,1	5,5	9,9	Statistical 5,5	Facades	Pater-nalism	Other
Thomas, W.I. & Znaniecki, F.	"Three Types of Personality." In C.W. Mills, ed., *Images of Man: The Classic Tradition in Sociological Thinking.* New York: George Braziller, Inc., 1960, pp. 405-436.	Sociology	427			407-408, 409,411, 418-419, 421,423, 425,427, 428,434, 435-436	408,409, 411,418, 423,435, 436	408-409, 418,423, 433,435, 436		420	
Wheelis, A.	*The Quest for Identity.* New York: W.W. Norton & Co., 1958.	Psychiatry	18,85			18-19, 48-49, 85-89, 91-93, 126	19,20	85			
White, R. & Lippitt, R.	"Leader Behavior and Member Reaction in Three 'Social Climates'." In D. Cartwright and A. Zander, eds., *Group Dynamics: Research and Theory.* (2nd ed.) Evanston, Ill.: Row, Peterson, & Co., 1960, pp. 527-553.	Social Psychology	528-529, 529-532, 537,540-541,541-546,549-553		528-529, 530,531, 533-534, 539-540, 549-552	528-529, 530,531, 532-538, 539-541, 546-549, 549-553					

*Reproduced by permission from Robert R. Blake and Jane S. Mouton. *"The Grid as a Comprehensive Framework for Analyzing Human Relationships."* Austin, Texas: Scientific Methods, Inc., 1977.

INDEX

D

E

F

M

N

O

P

Q

R